Letters
To
Young
Black
Women

Other Books

by
Daniel Whyte III

- *LETTERS TO YOUNG BLACK MEN*

- *MO' LETTERS TO YOUNG BLACK MEN*

- *WHEN BLACK PREACHERS PREACH, Volume I,*
  Editor

- *WHEN BLACK PREACHERS PREACH, Volume II,*
  Editor

- *WHEN BLACK PREACHERS PREACH, Volume III,*
  Editor

- *MONEY UNDER THE CAR SEAT (AND OTHER
  THINGS TO THANK GOD FOR)*

- *7 THINGS YOUNG BLACK MEN DO TO MESS UP
  THEIR LIVES*

- *7 THINGS YOUNG BLACK WOMEN DO TO MESS
  UP THEIR LIVES*

- *GOD HAS SMILED ON ME: A TRIBUTE TO A
  BLACK FATHER WHO STAYED*

- *JUST JESUS!: THE GREATEST THINGS EVER SAID
  ABOUT THE GREATEST MAN WHO EVER LIVED,*
  Editor

Letters to Young Black Women

Loving, Fatherly Advice and Encouragement for a Difficult Journey

by
Daniel Whyte III
with Meriqua & Daniella Whyte

LETTERS TO YOUNG BLACK WOMEN

Cover Design by Bill Hopper of Hopper Graphics.

© Copyright 2006
TORCH LEGACY PUBLICATIONS, DALLAS, TEXAS;
ATLANTA, GEORGIA; BROOKLYN, NEW YORK

First Printing, 2006

The Bible quotations in this volume are from the King James Version of the Bible.

The name TORCH LEGACY PUBLICATIONS and its logo are registered as a trademark in the U.S. patent office.

ISBN: 0-9763487-6-4

Printed in the USA.

This book is lovingly dedicated to

My daughters:

Daniella, Danita, Danielle, Danae`, Daniqua and
Danyelle,

My granddaughter, Kywaizia,

My wife, Meriqua,

My Mother, Shirley Louise White,

My Mother-in-Law, Hermoth Keturah Dixon

My sisters:

Sheila Martin, Temolynn Wintons, Diane Dixon,
and Stephanie White

My sons:

Daniel IV, Duran and Danyel Ezekiel,

who I hope will find good young black women to marry,
if that is God's will for their lives,

And to

All young black women in America and
around the world.

In loving memory
of two
classy black ladies
who are now
forever young:

Rosa Parks
&
Coretta Scott-King

Letters to Young Black Women

CONTENTS

PART III: On Your Life – As A Young Black Woman

ACKNOWLEDGMENTS

*F*irst of all, I wish to thank God for allowing me the joy and privilege to do such a work as this. I also wish to thank the readers of the book *Letters to Young Black Men*, who encouraged me to write this book.

I would like to thank my wife, Meriqua, and my daughter, Daniella, for helping me to write this book; my son, Daniel IV for his hard work, advice, and for typesetting this book; my daughters, Danita, Danae`, and Daniqua, for helping to find the quotations and creating the prayers contained in this book; and my two youngest children, Danyel Ezekiel and Danyelle Elizabeth for being good children while I worked on this project.

I must especially thank Dr. Melissa Russell, adjunct professor of Languages and Literature at Texas Wesleyan University, for editing the manuscript, and for her encouragement; Charles and Ruth Garrett for proofreading the manuscript, and for being a continuous source of encouragement and support; Bill Hopper of Hopper Graphics for doing such an awesome job on the cover, and for just being a great brother in Christ; Pete Hoelzl, Stella Cazares and their fine staff for believing in us and doing such a great job in printing the book; Ron Smith and Edna Byrd of Bookworld Companies, as well as John Bomberger and Simon Schrock of Choice Books, for having the confidence in our publishing company to take us on and who encouraged us to move forward on this project as well as others. May God bless all of the people, named and unnamed, who were a part in producing this volume.

Letters to Young Black Women

INTRODUCTION

"The true worth of a race must be measured by the character of its womanhood."
—Mary McLeod Bethune

I am forever amazed at the broad shoulders of black women, and how God has used them down through the years in this country and beyond, to not only help the black community stay together, but to move us forward as a race — yea, indeed, to even help hold America together, and to move her forward as well.

I think about the courage of Harriett Tubman, Ida B. Wells, and Sojourner Truth. I also think about the class, dignity, and toughness of Coretta Scott-King, Rosa Parks and Dorothy Height. I am afraid, however, that these women had something that many of our young black women today simply do not have.

I am very concerned for our young black women. In light of the quote above by Mary McLeod Bethune, *"The true worth of a race must be measured by the character of its womanhood,"* many of our young women today are not expressing the character and the class that the black women of old showed. Many of them have dropped the standards of the past. I remember even when I was a child back in the sixties and seventies, when the young ladies were admonished by the grandmothers, mothers, and aunts to "stop being so fast": a clear warning that meant to stop carrying yourself like a loose girl. It meant to stop running after boys and to carry yourself like a lady. Well, I haven't heard that phrase in a long time, and unfortunately, it is showing. Consider with me some horrifying statistics regarding our young women today:

- The African-American teen birth rate remains at 85.3 births per 1,000 women.

- The pregnancy rate of young black women 15-19 years old is twice that of whites.

- The average number of abortions performed on black women every day in the United States is 1,500.

- 41,743 African-American women are in prison; 95,308 are on probation; 23,916 are on parole; 2,962 are in jail; and 81,996 are ex-felons.

- The school dropout rate for African American women is 11%.

Besides the painful facts above, what troubles me the most is that more young black women today are allowing themselves to be used, mistreated, and hurt by unscrupulous men who do not care anything for them, and who do not even have the capacity to treat them with love and respect. And what happens is that moral failures that are pleasurable and seem small while doing them, end up impacting the rest of their lives with devastating consequences. I believe this lack of self-respect is what breeds the horrifying statistics above.

This book is more about prevention than it is about healing. There are many other great men and women of God who are doing great work in the healing and restoration department for young black women. (We mention some of these individuals and ministries on our "Motherboard" in the back of the book.) I believe that many of the problems that you, as young black women are dealing with today can be prevented from happening in the first place. I also believe that in order for you to be victorious in this life, you must operate from a position of strength and power based upon the Word of God. This book will empower you to win against your enemies: the devil, sorry men, and even yourself. I hope that you will read it and never live a defeated life again.

If Black America is to survive and thrive, not only do our young black men need to rise, but our young black women need to rise again.

—*Daniel Whyte* **III**
Irving, Texas

"Women, if the soul of the nation is to be saved, I believe that you must become its soul."

–Coretta Scott-King

"NEVER UNDERESTIMATE A YOUNG BLACK WOMAN."

—Daniel Whyte III

"NEVER GIVE UP ON A YOUNG BLACK WOMAN — BECAUSE YOU NEVER KNOW..."

—Daniel Whyte III

"TO BLACK MEN: NEVER AGAIN NEGLECT, MISTREAT, ABUSE OR HURT A YOUNG BLACK WOMAN, BECAUSE SHE WILL NEVER FORGET WHAT YOU DID TO HER."

—Daniel Whyte III

"IF YOU CONSIDER YOURSELF YOUNG, MA'AM, THEN YOU ARE YOUNG."

—Daniel Whyte III

ON YOUR LIFE
—SPIRITUAL

FROM MY HEART

Letter One

Dear Daughters & YBW:

These letters are written with a full heart, yea, a heart overflowing. What I mean by that is this: I have shared these thoughts and principles with my daughters for years in the presence of my wife, Meriqua. These letters are addressed first to my daughters, and I am just going to open a vein and bleed these loving truths out to you as well.

As I begin writing this letter, I am reminded of a book title I read some time ago by the famed Southern author, Lewis Grizzard; it read: *Elvis is Dead and I Don't Feel So Good Myself.* Grizzard's book title aptly describes my current condition, because you see, I now lie in a hospital bed under observation for chest pains, and, as I dictate this book to my daughter, Daniella, I think of Coretta Scott-King's funeral to be held tomorrow, and Rosa Parks' funeral that was held just a few days ago.

I strongly believe that with the passing of these two great women is the passing of an era of great black women. Very few women, black or white, today, carry themselves with such high standards, class and dignity.

I hope that you, young dear sisters, will follow the example of these great women and walk in their footsteps to bring back the standards of old that America so desperately needs.

In order to begin to do that, you have to **Let God Touch You**, and that is what I will deal with in my next letter.

From My Heart,

Papa

P.S.: Throughout this book, I will refer to Young Black Women as **"YBW."** The information contained after my letters are some things that you can take with you throughout your life. Instead of calling them **P.S.'s,** they will be called **P.T.'s for "Power-Thoughts."**

P.T. (Power-Thoughts):

♦ *"When I stand before God at the end of my life, I would hope that I would not have a single bit of talent left, and could say, 'I used everything you gave me.'"*
—Erma Bombeck

BIBLE GEM: "Take fast hold of instruction; let her not go: keep her; for she is thy life." *—Proverbs 4:13*

TALK TO GOD: Lord Jesus, as I read these letters, help me to have an open heart and an open ear to receive Your words of truth and love. Help me to apply all that I read to my life and to be the woman that You want me to be. In Jesus Christ's precious name. Amen.

BOOK: He Speaks To Me: Preparing to Hear From God, by Priscilla Shirer

CHECK IT OUT: www.priscillaspeaks.com

LET GOD TOUCH YOU

Letter Two

Dear Daughters & YBW:

I want you to know that you are a special blessing from God. As far as I am concerned, the greatest gift to God's green earth has been women. God has blessed you to be a woman. In my opinion, without you, this world would be incomplete and colorless. Without a woman, the Son of God would have never been born. So, I must join T.D. Jakes in saying, "God loves His girls." The world may be hostile towards you, but God loves you very much, and you need to keep that in your heart and mind throughout the vicissitudes of life.

In this, my second letter to you, I want to encourage you to let God touch you — deeply. For some reason, traditionally, women have been more attracted to the Lord than men have been. The first people to the tomb were women; many of Jesus' followers were women. If you are not a follower of His, you need to get to know Him for yourself. In order to do that, you must open up your heart to Him, and let Him touch you. Well, you say, how do I do that? I'm glad you asked.

I was raised in the church, but I got saved outside of the church because I never heard a clear, understandable, presentation of the Gospel of the Lord Jesus Christ while in the church. So, listen closely to what I'm about to tell you:

First of all, **understand that you are a sinner like the rest of us.** Yes, believe it or not, each one of us born into this world has sinned. All of us have broken the laws of God. The Bible states plainly:

"For all have sinned and come short of the glory of God."
—Romans 3:23

Second, **God wants us to understand that because of our sin, there is a great punishment and that punishment is death — both spiritual death and physical death**. You see, because of sin, we die physically, but also because of sin, we die spiritually. This spiritual death is actually eternal separation from God in a place called Hell. Notice what God's Word says about this death in Romans 6:23: *"For the wages of sin is death…"*

Also consider the following verse from Revelation 21:8:

"But the fearful, and unbelieving, and the abominable, and murderers, and whoremongers, and sorcerers, and idolaters, and all liars, shall have their part in the lake which burneth with fire and brimstone: which is the second death."

Third, **after realizing our sad and condemned condition, God wants us to understand that He loves us more than we love ourselves**. He loves us so much that He sent His only Son, Jesus Christ, to live, suffer, shed His blood, and die on Calvary's cross for your sin and mine. After Jesus' earth-shaking death that day, He was buried and three days later He rose by the power of God.

Consider the following verse from John 3:16: *"For God so loved the world, that He gave His only begotten Son, that whosoever believeth in him should not perish, but have everlasting life."*

In order to really know God, you must go through His only begotten Son, Jesus Christ. Notice what Jesus Christ said about Himself: *"I am the way, the truth, and the life: no man cometh unto the Father, but by me"* (John 14:6).

Jesus Christ is the only way to God. Jesus Christ is the only way to joy, peace, and to eternal life. Here is how to accept Him into your heart according to the Scriptures:

"That if thou shalt confess with thy mouth the Lord Jesus, and shalt believe in thine heart that God hath raised him from the dead, thou shalt be saved."

—Romans 10:9

"For whosoever shall call upon the name of the Lord shall be saved."

—Romans 10:13

Dear YBW, if you want to know God, the source of all love, joy, peace, real happiness and true success, believe in your heart that Jesus Christ died, was buried, and rose again for you, and ask Him to come into your heart and save you. He will. You have God's Word on it.

Yours for Letting God Touch You,

P.T.:

♦ *"If we open our hearts to God, He has promised to work within us."* —Prime Min. Margaret Thatcher

♦ *"The knowledge of sin is the beginning of salvation."* —Epicurus

♦ *"The spiritual part of you can be thought of as the part of you that cannot be seen with the natural eye. This part of you will live forever. And where the spiritual you lives, depends on the decision you make today."* —Joyce Meyer

♦ *"The cross is the only ladder high enough to touch Heaven's threshold."* —G.D. Boardman

♦ *"A man may go to heaven without health, without riches, without honors, without learning, without friends, but he can never go there without Christ."* —John Dyer

BIBLE GEM: "...There is joy in the presence of the angels of God over one sinner that repenteth."

—Luke 15:10

TALK TO GOD: Lord Jesus, I know that I am a sinner and that I have broken your commandments. I now believe with all my heart that you — Jesus Christ, died, was buried, and rose on the third day. I am now ready for you to become the Lord of my life. Please come into my heart and save my soul and live within me forever. Thank you for your love and for your forgiveness. In Jesus Christ's precious name, I pray. Amen!

BOOK: The God I Love: A Lifetime of Walking with Jesus, by Joni Eareckson Tada

CHECK IT OUT : www.torchlegacy.com/ throughthedoor

LET GOD HEAR FROM YOU

Letter Three

Dear Daughters & YBW:

Yes, it is true: God loves His girls in a very special way, and He desires to hear from you regularly. Why does God want to hear from you? Well, He wants to hear from you for several reasons:

1. He loves you, and He created you to fellowship with Him.

2. He knows that you need Him. He wants to guide you and to direct you to success in life.

3. He wants you to have wisdom and obtain favor in the sight of God and man.

4. He wants to bless your life with the things you need and the good things you desire.

Please notice what the Bible says in Jeremiah 33:3: *"Call unto me, and I will answer thee, and shew thee great and mighty things which thou knowest not."*

One of the reasons why I am emphasizing prayer early in this book is because in my life experience, many women have a hard time maintaining a solid prayer life. Take for example, my wife of 20 years, Meriqua. I recall that when we first got married, for several months when I attempted to pray with her, she really didn't want to pray, and she would fall asleep while praying. The truth is, my new Christian bride was simply not as interested in prayer as I was. Not only that, but she also didn't really see the importance of prayer. Prayer is just as important for women as it is for men. If you have a hard time praying as well, here's how to get started:

- **How To Pray:** In praying, follow the example our Lord Jesus Christ laid down in Matthew 6:9-13:

    a. Thank the Lord (verse 9)
    b. Ask God's will for your life (verse 10)
    c. Ask for your daily needs (verse 11)
    d. Confess your sins and ask for forgiveness (verse 12)
    e. Ask God to deliver you from temptation, evil, and sin (verse 13a)
    f. Praise the Lord (verse 13b)

- **When To Pray:** Pray as the Lord leads you. The Holy Spirit will prompt you to pray throughout the day. It is also good to pray at appointed times, as King David and the Prophet Daniel did. The Bible says in I Thessalonians 5:17 that we ought to, *"Pray without ceasing."*

May I lovingly encourage you to overcome any obstacle that would hinder you from maintaining a strong prayer life? Prayer does not have to be difficult. Just keep it simple, to the point, and remember what the great author and evangelist John R. Rice used to say: "Prayer is simply asking and receiving from God." Regular, consistent communication with God Almighty will make all the difference in your life.

"Pray without ceasing." —Apostle Paul

With Love and Prayer,

P.T.:

♦ *"God is more interested in the quality of the prayer, not the quantity and eloquence of the words."*
—Anonymous

♦ *"Prayer is a Sin-Killer. No one can sin and pray, for prayer will either make us cease from sin, or sin will make us cease from prayer."*
—Anonymous

♦ *"Any concern too small to be turned into a prayer is too small to be made into a burden."*
—Corrie ten Boom

♦ *"Do not have your concert first and tune your instruments afterward. Begin the day with God."*
—J. Hudson Taylor

♦ *"When the 'prayers' go up, the blessings come down."*
—Daniel Whyte III

BIBLE GEM: "Ask, and it shall be given you; seek, and ye shall find; knock, and it shall be opened unto you."
—Matthew 7:7

TALK TO GOD: Lord Jesus, thank you for giving me the privilege of prayer. I pray that you would help me to be a woman of prayer and help me to learn to depend on You for everything. In Jesus Christ's name. Amen.

BOOK: *The Prayer That Changes Everything: The Hidden Power of Praising God,* by Stormie Omartian

CHECK IT OUT: www.liveprayer.com

LET GOD TALK TO YOU

Letter Four

Dear Daughters & YBW:

I trust that you are doing well today.

In this letter, I want to encourage you to let God talk to you. What I mean by this is, I want you to get into the habit of reading the Word of God — the Bible — on a regular basis. Let the Word of God be your guide — not popular opinion, not your girlfriends, not your emotions, but the Word of God. Be a woman of the Word! Frankly, there is nothing more beautiful on God's green earth than a woman who lives by the Word of God, and not by her feelings and emotions. Men are attracted to her, women respect her and listen to her, and children love her. The Bible refers to this woman as a virtuous woman — whose *"price is far above rubies"* (Proverbs 31:10). In other words, you cannot put a price on such a woman.

I strongly encourage you to make it a daily habit to read the Word of God, to study the Word of God, to meditate on the Word of God, and to live by the Word of God. Reading and doing the Word of God, young sister, will keep you from a lot of pain and heartache in this life. Psalm 119:11 says: *"Thy word have I hid in mine heart, that I might not sin against thee."* When you put the Word of God in your heart, your conscience will not allow you to linger in sin. The great preacher, D.L. Moody, once said, "This Book will keep you away from sin or sin will keep you away from this Book." Reading and doing the Word of God will make you a smart and wise woman; it will make you a leader instead of a follower.

Notice what these women said about the Word of God:

> **"Scripture has phenomenal power, but unless you submit your mind to its inerrant truth, its power is largely lost to you."**
>
> —Martha Kilpatrick

> **"The Word of God is a Person. When you read it, do you see words or do you see Him?"**
>
> —Jacquelyn K. Heasley

> **"That Book [the Bible] accounts for the supremacy of England."**
>
> —Queen Victoria

Again, let me strongly encourage you to love, cherish, read, meditate on and obey the Word of God, because, if you do so, it will make you a woman who is priceless.

With the Bible in my Heart & Hand,

Papa

P.T.:

♦ *"Study the Bible through. Never begin a day without mastering a verse from its pages. Pray it in. Never lay aside your Bible until the verse or passage you have studied has become part of your being. Put it down. The thoughts that God gives you put down in*

44

the margin of your Bible or in your notebook. **Work it out.** Live the truth you get in the morning through each hour of the day. **Pass it on.** Seek to tell somebody else what you have learned."

—J. Wilbur Chapman

♦ "What makes the difference is not how many times you have been through the Bible, but how many times and how thoroughly the Bible has been through you."

—Gipsy Smith

♦ "The Bible is God's mirror which shows man as he is — not as he thinks he is!"

—Selected

BIBLE GEM: "Study to shew thyself approved unto God, a workman that needeth not to be ashamed, rightly dividing the word of truth."

—2 Timothy 2:15

TALK TO GOD: Dear God, thank you for Your Holy Word. Give me understanding as I read it through, but above all, help me to obey it and to hide it away in my heart. In Jesus Christ's precious name. Amen.

BOOK: *Believing God,* by Beth Moore

CHECK IT OUT: www.annegrahamlotz.com

LET GOD LOVE YOU

Letter Five

Dear Daughters & YBW:

I really want you to understand that God loves you. He really does. Now, I am not just saying that. Rather, I really want you to get it because so many young women have messed up their lives seeking love in the wrong places.

According to I John 4:8: *"God is love."* True love emanates from God. This love is called *agape* love, which is unconditional and unselfish love. His love accepts you just as you are. May I encourage you to bask in the love of God?

Here's how you can enjoy the love of God:

First, **you must understand that God loves you so much that He will never forsake you**. *"For he hath said, I will never leave thee, nor forsake thee"* (Hebrews 13:5b). Remember once you trust Christ as Saviour, you will always be His Child. God's love will never fail you. It has never failed me, and it won't fail you either.

Second, **you must keep your mind on God.** The Bible says in Isaiah 26:3: *"Thou wilt keep him in perfect peace, whose mind is stayed on thee: because he trusteth in thee."* If you want to enjoy the love and peace of God throughout your life, keep your mind on God all day, every day.

Third, another way to enjoy the love of God is to **stay in constant contact with Him.** Consider with me the following verses that encourage us to stay in touch with God:

"Pray <u>without ceasing</u>."

—I Thessalonians 5:17

"Praying <u>always</u> with all prayer and supplication in the Spirit, and watching thereunto with all perseverance and supplication for all saints."

—Ephesians 6:18

"Men ought <u>always</u> to pray, and not to faint."

—Luke 18:1

Fourth, another way to enjoy the love of God is to **make sure you don't break fellowship with him through disobedience and sin.** *"If we say that we have fellowship with him, and walk in darkness, we lie, and do not the truth: But if we walk in the light, as he is in the light, we have fellowship one with another, and the blood of Jesus Christ his Son cleanseth us from all sin"* (I John 1:6 & 7).

Fifth, another great way to enjoy the love of God is by **sharing His love with others**. The Lord commissions us, as His children, to share His love with others in what is called "the Great Commission." *"Go ye therefore, and teach all nations, baptizing them in the name of the Father, and of the Son, and of the Holy Ghost: Teaching them to observe all things whatsoever I have commanded you: and, lo, I am with you alway, even unto the end of the world. Amen"* (Matthew 28:19-20).

If you want to share God's love with others, here's a quick and easy way to do it:

A. Help them to understand that according to the Bible, we are all sinners, and that we all deserve punishment in Hell. Show them Romans 3:23 and Romans 6:23.

B. Tell them that God loves them so much that He sent Jesus Christ to die on the cross for their sins. Show them John 3:16.

C. Tell them that they must trust Jesus Christ to save them. Show them Romans 10:9 & 13.

YBW, bask in the love of God throughout your life, and be the happy, peaceful, powerful, vibrant, Christian woman that God wants you to be.

Loved by God,

Papa

P.T.:

♦ *"Does God love us because we are special — or are we special because God loves us?"*
—William Arthur Ward

♦ *"I am radically, insanely, nutty in love with Jesus! He has set me free!"*
—Joyce Meyer

♦ *"Love conquers all."*
—Virgil

♦ "When you have nothing left but God, then for the first time you become aware that God is enough."
—Maude Royden

♦ "The loneliest place in the world is the human heart when love is absent."
—E. C. McKenzie

BIBLE GEM: "And to know the love of Christ, which passeth knowledge, that ye might be filled with all the fullness of God."
—Ephesians 3:19

TALK TO GOD: Holy Father God, I thank You so much for Your love. I pray that You would help me to keep Your love in my heart at all times and to share it with others. In the precious name of Jesus Christ I pray. Amen.

BOOK: *Loving God with All Your Mind,* by Elizabeth George

CHECK IT OUT: www.lorri.com

LET GOD BE YOUR ALL IN ALL

Letter Six

Dear Daughters & YBW:

I trust that you are doing well today. I am doing fine.

As you go through this life, you will find many times that the only Person you can depend on in times of trouble is God. People who you thought were your friends will forsake you, but God has assured us in His Word that He will *"never leave thee, nor forsake thee"* (Hebrews 13:5). So, in this letter, I want to share with you how to let God be your main source — your all in all — in this life:

First, **you must be totally dependent upon God.** Proverbs 3:5 & 6 tells us to *"Trust in the Lord with all thine heart; and lean not unto thine own understanding. In all thy ways acknowledge him, and he shall direct thy paths."* Throughout my life, I have found it to be the case, that when I put God first in everything and when I totally depend on Him, He has always led me in the right path and brought me through every difficulty that I have faced.

Second, **you must be fully committed to God.** The Bible says in Romans 12:1: *"I beseech you therefore, brethren, by the mercies of God, that ye present your bodies a living sacrifice, holy, acceptable unto God, which is your reasonable service."* You must make up your mind to be totally committed to God, no matter what. When God sees that you have given your all in all, He has a way of bestowing upon you all kinds of blessing and favor. This is why I believe the Bible said, "David was a man after God's own heart." David was totally committed to God. Be committed to the Lord throughout your life and be a woman after God's own heart.

Third, **you must completely surrender your will to God's.** Your daily prayer should be the same as Jesus' when He was in the garden of Gethsemane, ***"Not my will, but thine be done"*** (Luke 22:42). When you are completely sold-out to God's will for your life, then you begin to make God your all in all.

Daughters and YBW, may I lovingly encourage you to let God be everything to you. Depend on Him, be committed to Him, surrender your will to His, and be the joyful, powerful, Christian woman that He wants you to be.

With God as My All in All,

P.T.:

♦ *"Looking back — Praise Him*
Looking ahead — Trust Him
Looking around — Serve Him
Looking up — Expect Him!"

—Selected

♦ *"The strength of a man (woman) consists in finding out the way God is going, and going that way."*
—Henry Ward Beecher

♦ "To walk out of God's will is to step into nowhere."
—C.S. Lewis

♦ "God will be present, whether asked or not."
—Latin Proverb

♦ "God never worries about being enough or having enough, because, after all, God is not only in everything, God is everything."
—Bob Lively

BIBLE GEM: "Thus saith the Lord the King of Israel, and his redeemer the Lord of hosts; I am the first, and I am the last; and beside me there is no God."
—Isaiah 44:6

TALK TO GOD: Lord Jesus, help me to trust in You and to serve You with all my heart, soul, and mind. Help me to rest in Your promises. And I pray that You would be in my thoughts always. In Jesus Christ's precious name. Amen.

BOOK: A Woman after God's Own Heart, by Elizabeth George

CHECK IT OUT: www.elizabethgeorge.com

LET GOD MAKE YOU A WOMAN OF FAITH

Letter Seven

Dear Daughters & YBW:

I trust that you are allowing God to be everything to you in these trying times.

Over the years, God has honored our faith in Him and has worked countless miracles for my family and me. I am reminded of a time, one Thanksgiving, years ago, when we did not have much money, and we were very low on food. But through prayer and faith in God, the Lord provided for us that Thanksgiving, not just one, but five turkeys, and much more. Let me encourage you to *"Have faith in God"* (Mark 11:22).

You may ask, well, how can I have a strong faith in God?

The first key to having a strong faith in God is to **spend quality time in prayer**. Prayer and faith go hand in hand because you cannot pray effectively without faith. It takes a strong faith to pray to a God you cannot see, for *"Without faith it is impossible to please him: for he that cometh to God must believe that he is, and that he is a rewarder of them that diligently seek him"* (Hebrews 11:6).

The second key to having a strong faith in God, is **reading and believing God's Word — the Bible**. Romans 10:17 says: *"So then faith cometh by hearing, and hearing by the Word*

55

of God." If you want to become a woman of faith, you will not only read God's Word and believe God's Word, but you will also obey God's Word. ***"But be ye doers of the Word, and not hearers only, deceiving your own selves"*** (James 1:22).

Daughters and YBW, may I lovingly encourage you to have a strong faith in God in these trying times. God will greatly bless you for it, and it will make all of the difference in your life.

Be a Woman of Faith,

Papa

P.T.:

♦ *"Faith is not belief. Belief is passive. Faith is active."*
                                                    —Edith Hamilton

♦ *"Prayer is the key to Heaven, but faith unlocks the door."*   *—Anonymous*

BIBLE GEM: "And Jesus answering saith unto them, Have faith in God."   *—Mark 11:22*

TALK TO GOD: Lord Jesus, make me into a woman of faith, to be used for Your glory, praise, and honor. In the majestic name of Jesus Christ. Amen.

BOOK: Matters of the Heart: Stop Trying to Fix the Old, Let God Give You Something New, by Juanita Bynum

CHECK IT OUT: www.womenoffaith.com

LET GOD MAKE YOU BEAUTIFUL FROM THE INSIDE OUT

Letter Eight

Dear Daughters & YBW:

At the writing of this note, I am alone in my recliner thinking of how God has blessed me with beautiful and healthy children. I really thank the Lord for each one of you, and for the natural beauty that He has given to each of you.

Even though I think that your mother is a beautiful woman, I have had to talk with her from time to time about things that make her ugly. These things make all people ugly, no matter how pretty they are. What are some of the things that make us ugly?

1. **Lying and Dishonesty.** At the top of the list is lying. Sweethearts, nothing will make you uglier in the sight of people than telling lies and being dishonest. Tell the truth no matter how much it might hurt. The Bible says in Proverbs 12:19: *"The lip of truth shall be established for ever: but a lying tongue is but for a moment."* Yes, the old adage is true: "HONESTY IS THE BEST POLICY."

2. **A Bad Spirit and Attitude.** Contrary to what so many people believe, I believe that we can control our attitudes and our spirits. The Bible states in Proverbs 25:28 that: *"He that hath no rule over his own spirit is like a city that is broken*

57

down, and without walls."

In other words, I believe that by a simple decision, we can control our attitudes and our spirits, no matter what the circumstances, and no matter how we feel physically or emotionally. Your moods and your feelings should not rule how you respond to your family, friends, and others. Have a sweet, beautiful spirit, and people will love to be around you.

3. **An Uncontrollable Tongue.** Now, my dad, Daniel Whyte, Jr., was the most loving man that I have ever met, but I can still hear him, hollering from the back room, from time to time, to my mother when they were fussing back and forth about something, "Shirley, your mouth is going to get your behind in trouble." Oh! How many people have allowed their uncontrollable tongues to get them in trouble. The Bible speaks about this in the book of James:

> *"And the tongue is a fire, a world of iniquity: so is the tongue among our members, that it defileth the whole body, and setteth on fire the course of nature; and it is set on fire of hell...But the tongue can no man tame; it is an unruly evil, full of deadly poison."*
> —James 3: 5 & 8

Oh! How terrible is a lying tongue. Oh! How terrible is a bad attitude and spirit. Oh! How terrible is an uncontrollable tongue. Sweethearts, choose to tell the truth, the whole truth, and nothing but the truth at all times. Determine to have a cheerful and joyful spirit at all times and in all circumstances. And choose by the grace of God to control your tongue in every situation. If you do so, you will be beautiful from the inside out.

Lovingly Yours for Being Beautiful from the Inside Out,

Papa

P.T.:

♦ *"It is not enough to be good if you have the ability to be better."*
                                        —*Alberta Lee Cox*

♦ *"Sometimes when we're waiting for God to speak, He's waiting for us to listen."*
                                        —*Martha Bolton*

BIBLE GEM: "Keep thy tongue from evil, and thy lips from speaking guile."
                                        —*Psalm 34:13*

TALK TO GOD: Dear Lord, please help me to be beautiful from the inside out. Fill me with Your grace, love, and mercy. I thank You for Your help. In Jesus Christ's name, I pray. Amen.

BOOK: The Princess Within: Restoring the Soul of a Woman, by Serita Ann Jakes

CHECK IT OUT: www.cecewinans.com

LET GOD CONTROL YOU

Letter Nine

Dear Daughters & YBW:

I am writing this letter from the Gospel Light Bible Baptist Church in Dallas, Texas. I trust that you are doing well.

Since I have started writing these letters to you, several things should have happened in your life: God should have touched you with salvation through Jesus Christ; God should be hearing from you through prayer; God should be speaking to you through His Word; God should be filling your life with love; God should be your all in all; God should be making you into a woman of faith; and, God should be making you beautiful from the inside out.

In this letter, I want to lovingly share with you the importance of letting God control your life. Please notice with me this very powerful verse: ***"This is the word of the Lord...Not by might, nor by power, but by my spirit, saith the Lord of hosts"*** (Zechariah 4:6). The verse above is what I consider to be my life's verse. I am a firm believer that if God, through His Holy Spirit does not do it, it won't be done. In other words, if we want to see true success in our lives, God is the one who will make it happen, not us. So let me strongly encourage you here to be a woman who allows God to control her, lead her, and guide her by His Holy Spirit because that is where the power is.

The Holy Spirit is your friend and life long help. Consider

with me this verse from John 15:26: *"But when the Comforter is come, whom I will send unto you from the Father, even the Spirit of truth, which proceedeth from the Father, he shall testify of Me."* Consider also this verse in John 16:13: *"Howbeit when he, the Spirit of truth, is come, he will guide you into all truth: for he shall not speak of himself; but whatsoever he shall hear, that shall he speak: and he will shew you things to come."*

Notice in this verse that the Holy Spirit is here to comfort you and guide you throughout your life. If you walk in the power of the Holy Spirit, good things will be manifested in your life. The Bible calls these things the fruit of the spirit, which are: *"...love, joy, peace, longsuffering, gentleness, goodness, faith, meekness, temperance: against such there is no law"* (Galatians 5:22, 23). When you let God control your life through the power of the Holy Spirit, the God of the universe can make something beautiful out of your life, and then you can relish in His peace and victory.

With God in Control,

Papa

P.T.:

♦ *"Don't bother to give God instructions; just report for duty."*

—Corrie ten Boom

♦ *"The only way to have victory in our lives is to play by God's rules."*

—Joyce Meyer

♦ *"That we are alive today is proof positive that God has something for us to do today."*

—Lindsay

BIBLE GEM: "But the Comforter, which is the Holy Ghost...shall teach you all things."

—John 14:26

TALK TO GOD: *Lord God, I pray in the name of the Lord Jesus Christ that You would control every part of me. Help me to listen to You before I listen to any one else and to obey Your commandments always. In Jesus Christ's name. Amen.*

BOOK: *And We Are Changed — Encounters with a Transforming God,* by Priscilla Evans Shirer

CHECK IT OUT: *www.loisevans.org*

LET GOD ENCOURAGE YOU

Letter Ten

Dear Daughters & YBW:

I trust that this letter finds you doing well. As I write this letter, I am in my living room thinking of how I continually teach my daughters to encourage themselves in the Lord. That is just what I want to talk to you about today.

As I write this letter to you, I am greatly reminded of a story in I Samuel 30, which tells of David fighting against the Amalekites. After the Amalekites had taken the city of Ziklag, and had taken captive the women and the children, and had burned the city, David and his men found the city in total destruction. David's own family was taken, and his men talked of stoning him. The Bible says in verse six that David was *"greatly distressed"*; then it says, *"David encouraged himself in the Lord his God."*

Encourage yourself in the Lord! You are His child, and He will never let anything harm you. The Bible says in Isaiah 54:17 that *"No weapon that is formed against thee shall prosper; and every tongue that shall rise against thee in judgment thou shalt condemn. This is the heritage of the servants of the Lord, and their righteousness is of me, saith the Lord."*

In order to stay encouraged, you must strengthen yourself through prayer and build up your faith by reading the Word of God. Go to church regularly. God wants you to be involved in a good, Bible-believing church, for that is truly the encouragement place. Fellowship with other saints and allow them to encourage you in your spiritual journey.

Always look back to where God has brought you from, and thank Him for what He has done for you.

Encouraged by God,

Papa

P.T.:

♦ *"My faith instills in me a deep sense of humility and gratitude, reminding me how often I fall short and how much I need the Savior, and how thankful I am that God has done for us what we could not do for ourselves."*

—*Karen Hughes*

BIBLE GEM: "I can do all things through Christ which strengtheneth me."

—*Philippians 4:13*

TALK TO GOD: Lord Jesus, Help me to allow You to encourage me in this life. I know that You will never leave me nor forsake me. Help me to keep my mind on You and my trust in You. Keep leading me through Your Word. In Jesus Christ's wonderful name. Amen.

BOOK: Let Me Be a Woman, by Elisabeth Elliot

CHECK IT OUT: www.elisabethelliot.org

LET GOD BLESS AND MAKE YOU A SUCCESS

Letter Eleven

Dear Daughters & YBW:

I trust that you have been doing well since my last letter to you.

It breaks my heart to see so many defeated and discouraged young black women in the world today. One of the goals of this book is to show you how you can live a successful, blessed, and victorious life.

The people who are happiest and who are genuinely successful are those who are divinely blessed by God. Well, you ask, how can I be divinely blessed by God?

First of all, **God wants you to be obedient to Him**. Deuteronomy 11:26-28 says: *"Behold, I set before you this day a blessing and a curse; A blessing, if ye obey the commandments of the Lord your God, which I command you this day: And a curse, if ye will not obey the commandments of the Lord your God, but turn aside out of the way which I command you this day, to go after other gods, which ye have not known."*

In order to obtain the blessings of God, you must obey His commandments. If you disobey them, you will be cursed. I have learned that God is no respecter of persons. He never blesses disobedience: He never has, and He never will, but, He does bless those who are obedient to Him.

Second, **you must study and meditate on the Word of God**. It is vital to your success. All the knowledge you need for success in this life will be found in the Bible. Joshua 1:8 says, *"This book of the law shall not depart out of thy mouth; but thou shalt meditate therein day and night, that thou mayest observe to do according to all that is written therein: for then thou shalt make thy way prosperous, and then thou shalt have good success."*

Third, **obey your parents and those in authority over you**. Always respect them and love them, even though you may walk your own road as you get older. Ephesians 6:1-3 says: *"Children, obey your parents in the Lord, for this is right. Honour thy father and mother; which is the first commandment with promise; That it may be well with thee, and thou mayest live long on the earth."* The Bible also says in I Peter 5:5: *"Likewise, ye younger submit yourselves unto the elder."*

God wants you to be a grand success in this life. The road to genuine success is very simple, but not easy. As I mention above, be obedient to the Lord, which includes prayer; read and meditate on the Word of God; listen to and honor your parents; additionally, always tell the truth no matter what, and make up your mind to do whatever it takes to reach your God-given goals. Remember, true success in life is doing what God created and gifted you to do, and doing it well for His glory.

Blessed with Success,

Papa

P.T.:

♦ *"We are not women of the world. We are women of God. And women of God will be among the greatest heroines of the 21st century."*
— Sheri L. Dew

♦ *"There is one discouraging thing about the rules of success — they won't work unless you do."*
— Anonymous

♦ *"When we do what we can, God will do what we can't."*
— Anonymous

♦ *"May you be truly blessed to always glitter with a radiance that shines from deep within you."*
— Barbara Becker Holstein

BIBLE GEM: *"The blessing of the Lord, it maketh rich, and he addeth no sorrow with it."*
— Proverbs 10:22

TALK TO GOD: *Dear God, I want to be a success, and I want You to bless me so that I can be a blessing to others. Help me to do my best for You all of my life, and help me to obey You so that I will never have my blessings hindered. I thank You in advance for everything. In Jesus Christ's name. Amen.*

BOOK: *10 Spiritual Principles of Successful Women: Discovering Your Purpose, Vision, and Blessing,* by Victoria Lowe

CHECK IT OUT: www.juliomelara.com

ON YOUR LIFE – EDUCATIONAL

ON THE IMPORTANCE OF YOUR EARLY EDUCATION

Letter Twelve

Dear Daughters & YBW:

In this letter, I want to shift gears a little. I want to get off of spiritual matters and get onto the matters of the mind. In this letter, I want to talk to you about the importance of your early education. So many young people today do not take their early education seriously. When I talk about an early education, I am referring to the education one can gain from the age of eleven and upward. It is vital that you see the importance of education at an early age.

The value of getting a good education is all around us. God even addresses the importance of increasing knowledge in His Word. Notice Proverbs 1:5: *"A wise man (wise woman) will hear and will increase learning; and a man (woman) of understanding shall attain unto wise counsels."*

Proverbs 9:9 tells us: *"Give instruction to a wise man, and he will be yet wiser: teach a just man, and he will increase in learning."* So become wiser by increasing in knowledge.

Now, increasing in knowledge does not happen by osmosis. There are certain things that will help you in your early education:

First, **you must have an internal motivation to want to learn.** You must have a desire to learn. No one can put that in you. It's a heart thing. It's a made up mind that says: "I want to learn. I want to know about the world around me."

Second, **you must take responsibility for your learning.** Your teachers can teach until they are blue in the face, and your parents can fuss at you about taking your schooling seriously, but your education will not be to you what it should be until you take full responsibility for it.

Third, **realize and keep in mind that what you learn will help you in life.** It will help make life better for you. If you play around and waste your time in junior and senior high school, your actions will show up in college and in your life. If you go to college just to pass the time, you will have a hard time in the working world. Don't go to school to play. Go to school to learn, and be all that God wants you to be.

Yours for a Great Early Education,

Papa

P.T.:

♦ *"Education can polish men, but only the blood of Christ can cleanse them."*
—*Anonymous*

♦ *"I think education is the single most important issue in our country. If we can get that one thing right, if we can make sure every single child gets a great education, it will solve a lot of our other problems."*
—*Laura Bush*

♦ *"The classroom is a sanctuary."*
—Daniel Whyte III

♦ *"Education's purpose is to replace an empty mind with an open one."*
—Malcolm S. Forbes

♦ *"Whoever cares to learn will always find a teacher."*
—German Proverb

BIBLE GEM: *"For the Lord giveth wisdom: out of his mouth cometh knowledge and understanding."*
—Proverbs 2:6

TALK TO GOD: *Dear God, I want to learn all that I can for your glory and honor. Give me your knowledge and grace to study hard to show myself approved unto you. Most of all, teach me Your Word. I ask all of this in Jesus' precious name. Amen.*

BOOK: *Living Beyond Yourself: Exploring the Fruit of the Spirit,* by Beth Moore

CHECK IT OUT: *www.school-for-champions.com*

ON SETTING EDUCATIONAL GOALS

Letter Thirteen

Dear Daughters & YBW:

I trust that you have begun to take your education seriously.

Over the years, I have learned that if you do not set goals, you will not accomplish anything. In this letter I want to encourage you to set solid educational goals.

What I mean by setting educational goals is this: you have to look at where you are now and map out where you would like to be in the next four, ten or twenty years. Write your goals down, pray over them, and ask God to lead, guide, and direct you as you work toward those goals.

After setting some solid goals, stay focused. Keep your eyes on the degree that you are pursuing. You will meet some obstacles along the way, but you must work toward your goals no matter what your girlfriends, your family, or others may say. Mark Twain once said: "It's not the size of the dog in the fight; it's the size of the fight that's in the dog." That is so true.

Don't let money be an issue. There is more than one way to reach your goals:

1. Prayer
2. Work part-time if needed

3. Well-off family members
4. External study colleges
5. Junior or Community Colleges
6. Scholarships for good grades
7. Financial Aid and Student Loans

No matter what grade you're in, I want you to start setting your educational goals right now. Take a pen and paper, and write down exactly what you would like to be doing at the age of twenty-five. Now, write down exactly what courses need to be taken to reach that goal. After you have written those courses down, pursue your educational goals like a woman on a mission, and don't let anything or anybody stand in your way.

Proverbs 13:19 says: ***"The desire accomplished is sweet to the soul..."***

Yours for Reaching the Finish Line,

P.T.:

♦ *"The thing you set your mind on is the thing you ultimately become."*
—*Nathaniel Hawthorne.*

♦ *"The world stands aside to let anyone pass who knows where he is going."*
—*David Starr Jordan*

♦ *"Only as high as I reach can I grow,*
only as far as I seek can I go,
only as deep as I look can I see,
only as much as I dream can I be."
— Karen Ravn

♦ *"I believe a knowledge of the Bible without a college course is more valuable than a college course without a Bible."*
— William Lyon Phelps

♦ *"Goals are dreams with deadlines."*
— Diana Hunt

♦ *"Dreaming has its values, but never should it become a substitute for work that needs to be done."*
— Anonymous

BIBLE GEM: *"Get wisdom, get understanding: forget it not; neither decline from the words of my mouth."*
— Proverbs 4:5

TALK TO GOD: *Lord Jesus, Help me to set some solid goals for my life. Give me Your discipline and the mind to fight toward my goals for Your glory. In Jesus Christ's name. Amen.*

BOOK: *Unstoppable Women: Achieve Any Breakthrough Goal in 30 Days,* by Cynthia Kersey

CHECK IT OUT: www.unstoppable.net

ON GETTING YOUR DOCTORATE DEGREE BEFORE MARRIAGE

Letter Fourteen

Dear Daughters & YBW:

I trust that you are being blessed today.

I want to make a strong suggestion to you, a suggestion that I am sure will raise some eyebrows. And that is: **Get your Doctorate Degree in some field that you love and in which you are especially gifted before you marry**, if that is the Lord's will for your life.

Now, you know, I believe that people who desire to get married ought to marry young if possible. But young in my book is 25 or 26 years old, and believe it or not, you can obtain your Doctorate by that age, if you apply yourself.

Now before you get scared, let me say here that this is just a strong suggestion. If God wants you to marry before then, that will be O.K. too. But I think you will be better off, and happier, if you follow my advice.

Here are some of the benefits for you if you follow this suggestion:

1. You can concentrate on and focus on your studies without distraction. (By the way, if possible, I would

encourage you to not even work a job while in college.)

2. If you are pursuing a Doctorate Degree in a certain field, you will be running with bright and wise people — those who are going in the same direction as you are. God may very well have you to meet someone special in that group. Even if you don't meet that special someone, you will meet many good people, and make friends that will last a lifetime.

3. You will grow so much in that strange period between the ages of 17 and 25 or 26, and the gaining of a good, solid, strong education will only enhance that period and certainly the rest of your life.

4. As a female, if you choose to have a career, I believe having a Doctorate in your field gives you more options, and will allow you to obtain a good paying job that will let you have more control over your schedule and the environment in which you work. In other words, you won't have to take jobs that would be distasteful to you, or that would compromise the principles by which you live.

Just consider it and see how the Lord may lead you.

Yours for Higher Education,

P.T.:

♦ *"Education: being able to differentiate between what you do know and what you don't. It's knowing where to go to find out what you need to know; and it's knowing how to use the information once you get it."*
—William Feather

BIBLE GEM: "Whoso loveth instruction, loveth knowledge: but he that hateth reproof is brutish."
—Proverbs 12:1

TALK TO GOD: Lord Jesus, Help me to keep looking to You for the goals that You want me to reach. I know that I cannot do anything without You, so please give me Your leadership and guidance. Fill me with Your power and might, to touch the world with Your love. In Jesus Christ's holy name. Amen.

BOOK: A Woman's High Calling: Growth and Study Guide, by Elizabeth George

CHECK IT OUT: www.hbcuconnect.com

THE MARKS OF A TRULY EDUCATED WOMAN

Letter Fifteen

Dear Daughters & YBW:

I have long been impressed with the Spelman woman. Please take notice with me a part of the mission statement of Spelman College:

> "…Spelman promotes academic excellence in the liberal arts and develops the intellectual, ethical, and leadership potential of its students." (Spelman College 2005-2006 Catalog)

When you think about the Spelman woman, you think of class, dignity, and leadership. What makes a Spelman woman appear that way? What are the marks of a truly educated black woman?

1. A truly educated woman has the utmost respect and love for God and for His Holy Word.

2. An educated woman carries herself with dignity, class, and grace.

3. An educated woman carries herself with a humble, quiet grace, yet her presence is powerful.

4. An educated woman knows how to handle the natural aggressiveness of men with coolness,

calmness, and without losing any respect from them.

5. An educated woman knows how to think on her feet, and how to speak clearly in any situation.

6. An educated woman understands the power of her eyes, and she knows how to control her eyes.

7. An educated woman knows how to express her thoughts through writing.

8. An educated woman knows how to think like a man when she needs to, and at the same time be all woman.

9. An educated woman knows her field very well.

10. An educated woman knows how to make both men and women feel at ease in her presence without losing respect.

11. An educated woman is disciplined and tough-minded.

12. An educated woman is discerning enough to say "no" to a man who doesn't mean her any good.

Daughters and YBW, may I lovingly encourage you to be this kind of woman.

Yours for a Truly Educated Black Woman,

86

P.T.:

♦ *"No one can make you feel inferior without your consent."*

—*Eleanor Roosevelt*

♦ *"Sow an act, and you reap a habit;*
  sow a habit, and you reap a character;
  sow a character, and you reap a destiny."

—*G.D. Boardman*

♦ *"The person who knows 'how' will always have a job.*
  The person who knows 'why' will always be his boss."

—*Diane Ravitch*

BIBLE GEM: "The fear of the Lord is the instruction of wisdom; and before honor is humility."

—*Proverbs 15:33*

TALK TO GOD: Lord Jesus, I pray that You would make me to be a strong, smart woman. Make me to be a woman of class, dignity, and leadership. Give me Your grace to handle every situation in which I find myself. In Jesus Christ's precious name, I pray. Amen.

BOOK: Chicken Soup for the Woman's Soul, by Jack Canfield & Mark Victor Hansen

CHECK IT OUT: www.chickensoup.com

THE POWER OF READING

Letter Sixteen

Dear Daughters & YBW:

I want to encourage you to expand your mind by reading throughout your life.

I am ashamed to say this, but as a child, neither my parents nor my teachers pushed me to read. In fact, I did not read an entire book through until I was a grown man and had learned the awesome power of reading on my own.

Why you should read:

a. Reading helps you to think (as opposed to the television which dulls your mind).
b. Reading helps you to write and speak better.
c. Reading increases your vocabulary.
d. Reading takes you places mentally that you may never be able to go physically.
e. Reading helps you to become a more educated person.

What you should read:

1. The Holy Bible
2. The Christian classics
3. A good grammar book
4. An African-American history book
5. An American history book
6. A book on etiquette

7. A book on personal hygiene
8. The classics by both black and white authors
9. A good daily newspaper or news magazine
10. A pocket dictionary

Of course, there are some books from which you need to stay away from. All books, sad to say, are not good books. Stay away from books or magazines that are pornographic in nature. Also, stay away from books and magazines that deal with gossip and foolishness. This kind of reading material does not advance you; it only slows you down from reaching your goals. Let me touch on romance novels. I know that I am getting ready to get into a whole lot of trouble here, but as a young, single, Christian lady, you do not need to be reading erotic novels that will get you all stirred up in your passions, knowing that at this time in your life you cannot fulfill them. There are many good Christian-based novels out there today that glorify God, honor Christ, and teach great life lessons. Read those.

I encourage you to keep your mind occupied with reading good and wholesome books. Always keep a good book with you so that if you have to wait at the airport, or wait in the doctor's office, you can use that time wisely by reading. Another thing that I like to do is listen to audio books while I drive, instead of listening to music. What a wonderful, easy way to get a good read in.

Readers are Leaders,

Papa

P.T.:

♦ *"Be as careful of the books you read as of the company you keep, for your character will be influenced as much by the one as the other."*
                                                —Selected

♦ *"It is impossible, mentally and socially, to enslave a Bible reading people."*   —Horace Greeley

♦ *"Education has produced a vast population able to read but unable to distinguish what is worth reading, an easy prey to sensations and cheap appeals."*   —G.M. Trevelyan

♦ *"The whole world opened to me when I learned to read."*   —Mary McLeod Bethune

♦ *"A room without books is like a body without a soul."*
                                                —G.K. Chesterton

BIBLE GEM: *"Till I come, give attendance to reading, to exhortation, to doctrine."*
                                                —I Timothy 4:13

TALK TO GOD: *Dear Lord, Please help me to realize the power of reading. Help me to read more so that I can understand the wonderful world that You have made. Create within me a love for reading. Help me to read Your Holy Word and to understand it. In Jesus Christ's name. Amen.*

BOOK: *A Beginner's Guide to Reading the Bible,* by Craig Koester

CHECK IT OUT: <u>www.goodgirlbookclubonline.com</u>

STRIVE TO KNOW WHAT YOU WANT TO DO WITH YOUR LIFE AT AN EARLY AGE

Letter Seventeen

Dear Daughters & YBW:

If you are applying what you are reading in this book, you are on your way to a fulfilling, happy, and successful life.

I am troubled to see so many young women today with a confused look on their faces, and seemingly no direction in their lives. I attribute this problem to their not having a purpose for their lives, and therefore having no goals to work toward. This is a tragedy!

Personally, I believe that by the age of twelve or so, you ought to have some idea of what you want to do with your life. Stop right now and ask yourself, what is my passion in life? What am I most interested in? What would I like to do for the rest of my life? I am forever amazed at people who are thirty, thirty-five, and even forty years old, who do not have a clue as to what God put them here on earth to do. I am very happy for the success of Rick Warren's fine book, *The Purpose Driven Life*. However, it really pained me to meet grown men and women who have been Christians for years — I'm talking about forty, fifty, and sixty years old — who thought this book was the best thing since sliced bread, and who through this book finally found their purpose in life. I felt very sad for these dear people.

Sister, I don't want you to wait until you are forty or fifty years old before you find out what God would have you to do. So that you won't think that I am hating on Rick Warren's book, *The Purpose Driven Life,* I encourage you to read it NOW. In fact, you will see that I have recommended this book for you to read at the end of this letter.

Now, back to finding out the purpose for your life. You need to understand two important facts:

> **1. God put you on this earth to do something that no one else can do.**

> **2. God has given you certain gifts and talents to do what He made you to do.**

What God wants you to do is to find out what that "something" is, and to do it with all of your might. Don't look at what your girlfriends are doing, and don't look at what anyone else is doing. Pray to God, and seek the advice of your parents. You will be surprised at how much your parents know about the direction you should take in your life.

The most important thing you should do, of course, is pray. Pray and seek God's will for your life. King Solomon, the wisest man who ever lived, said in Proverbs 3:5 & 6: *"Trust in the Lord with all thine heart and lean not unto thine own understanding; in all thy ways acknowledge him and he shall direct thy paths."* If you bathe your dreams and aspirations in prayer, then you have God's Word that He will direct your ways.

After you find out from God what He would have you to do with your life, go to the library with your parents and start mapping out courses and colleges that will help you get the training you need to do the calling that God has placed upon your life. Instead of your teenage years being boring and confusing, they can be exciting and joyful because you have clear direction in life.

Strive to know what God would have you to do at an early age, spend your young years working towards those goals, and you will be amazed at how God will use your life.

Plan for the Future,

P.T.:

♦ *"The poorest of all men is not the man without a cent; it is the man without a dream."*
> —Anonymous

♦ *"Thinking is the hardest work there is, which is the probable reason so few engage in it."*
> —Henry Ford

♦ *"Don't wait to see what happens — take hold and make it happen."*
> —Selected

♦ "Take responsibility for yourself, because no one's going to take responsibility for you."

—Tyra Banks

♦ "Choose a job you love and you will never have to work a day in your life."

—Confucius

BIBLE GEM: "But continue thou in the things which thou hast learned and hast been assured of, knowing of whom thou hast learned them; And that from a child thou hast known the holy scriptures, which are able to make thee wise unto salvation through faith which is in Christ Jesus."

—2 Timothy 3:14-15

TALK TO GOD: Dear Jesus, Please give me direction for my life. Show me what You want me to do that will please You and that will lead others to You. Please help me to start working toward those goals and visions that You have for me now. I know that You made me for a specific purpose. Help me to fulfill that purpose. In Jesus Christ's glorious name. Amen.

BOOK: The Purpose Driven Life, by Rick Warren

CHECK IT OUT: www.purposedrivenlife.com

TAKE IN A LITTLE ETIQUETTE ALONG THE WAY

Letter Eighteen

Dear Daughters & YBW:

As you know, I hold women such as Coretta Scott King, Rosa Parks and Condoleezza Rice, as well as others, in high esteem. These women, along with others, carry and have carried themselves with dignity, class, and grace.

In this letter, I want to encourage you to learn a little etiquette as you pursue your education, for this will help you to be a well rounded person. You must know how to act in every situation. Sad to say, many schools do not teach etiquette, so, you have to have the inner drive to learn it for yourself.

Below are a few basic rules of etiquette:

1. Use words such as "Please," "Thank you," "No Sir," "Yes Sir," "No Ma'am," "Yes Ma'am." (By the way, you are not any less of a person when you use such terminology. All you are doing is showing respect for older people, and people in positions of authority.)
2. Say "Excuse me" when you need to pass by someone.
3. Say "Pardon me" or "Excuse me" when you need someone to repeat themselves.
4. As a female, when you are introduced to the opposite sex, if you do not wish to shake the gentleman's hand, you do not have to extend your hand first.

5. Stand and walk upright.
6. Do not slouch when you sit down. Always sit up straight.
7. When you are in the wrong, always say "I apologize for so and so; would you please forgive me?" Or, "I am sorry; would you please forgive me?" (These small things go a long way in life.)

Below are some books to help you in the area of etiquette:

Miss Manners:
Guide to Excruciating Correct Behaviour
By Judith Martin
(Atheneum)

Emily Post's Etiquette
By Peggy Post
(Collins)

Commonsense Etiquette: A Guide to Gracious, Simple
Manners for the Twenty-First Century
By Marjabelle Young Stewart
(St. Martin's Griffin)

A Guide to Elegance: For Every Woman Who Wants to be
Well and Properly Dressed on All Occasions
By Genevieve Antoine Dariaux
(William Morrow)

Throughout your life, you will be invited to different occasions, and you do not want to appear ignorant of the proper rules of society. Learn some simple rules of etiquette so that you can be prepared for any occasion.

Do the right thing,

Papa

P.T.:

♦ *"Cleanliness is next to Godliness."*

—*Selected*

♦ *"What does anxiety do? It does not empty tomorrow of its sorrow, but it empties today of its strength. It does not make you escape the evil; it makes you unfit to cope with it if it comes."*

—*Anonymous*

BIBLE GEM: *"For God hath not called us unto uncleanness, but unto holiness."*

—*I Thessalonians 4:7*

TALK TO GOD: *Lord Jesus, I pray that You would help me to carry myself like a Godly woman. Give me the dignity and grace to do so. In Jesus Christ's name. Amen.*

BOOK: *Better Than Beauty: A Guide to Charm,* by *Helen Valentine & Alice Thompson*

CHECK IT OUT: www.emilypost.com

USE YOUR EDUCATION TO HELP OTHER PEOPLE

Letter Nineteen

Dear Daughters & YBW:

I trust that you have already set your educational goals, and that you are pursuing them with all your might. However, let me lovingly encourage you to pursue your education not only to meet your own needs, but to glorify God and to help other people.

Don't allow yourself to become a person who is always taking in and never giving out. You know, why they call the Dead Sea, the Dead Sea? The Dead Sea is always taking in and never giving out. In other words, don't increase in knowledge and never use the knowledge you gain for God's glory and to help other people. You will become spiritually and mentally constipated.

You will become puffed up if you increase in knowledge yet never share that knowledge. The Bible says in I Corinthians 8:1 that *"...knowledge puffeth up, but charity edifieth."*

So, I want to encourage you to share your knowledge with others. Have an "others first" mentality. (Remember the acronym, J-O-Y, which means Jesus, Others, You.) God wants you to be a blessing to others. There is a verse in Proverbs 11:24 that says: *"There is that scattereth, and yet increaseth; and there is that withholdeth more than is meet, but it tendeth to poverty."* Verse 25 goes on to say: *"The liberal soul shall*

101

be made fat (prosperous): and he that watereth shall be watered also himself."

Below are just a few ways in which the Lord can use you to help others:

- ♦ engage in ministry work at your church or para-church ministry
- ♦ help tutor an elementary school child
- ♦ do volunteer work at your local hospice
- ♦ volunteer at the library
- ♦ work as a teacher's aid
- ♦ help an elderly person or a mother with children by cleaning their house
- ♦ cook a meal for a sick person
- ♦ help out at a day care center
- ♦ go grocery shopping for the elderly
- ♦ sponsor a child through World Vision
- ♦ donate your old clothes to a thrift store
- ♦ mentor a troubled teenage girl

Let God use you to be a blessing to other people. Love and care for other people. Reach out to someone even today. After you finish reading this letter, go and do something nice for an elderly person that you know who needs some help. Not only will it be a blessing to them, but you will be amazed at how much you will be blessed as well. Jesus said, *"It is more blessed to give than to receive"* (Acts 20:35).

Reach Out and Touch Someone,

P.T.:

♦ *"There are too many people who expect God to work by miracle what God expects people to work by muscle."*

—*W. Galloway Tyson*

♦ *"Think of something to give instead of something to get."* —*Anonymous*

♦ *"The fragrance always remains in the hand that gives the rose."*

—*Heda Bejar*

♦ *"No person was ever honored for what he received. Honor has been the reward for what he gave."*
—*Calvin Coolidge*

BIBLE GEM: **"She stretcheth out her hand to the poor; yea, she reacheth forth her hands to the needy."**
—*Proverbs 31:20*

TALK TO GOD: Father God, Help me to realize how much You have blessed me. Help me to use the talents that You have given me to reach out to someone else and to show them Your love. Use me for Your glory and honor. In Jesus Christ's name. Amen.

BOOK: 101 Ways to Help People in Need, by Steve & Janie Sjogren

CHECK IT OUT: www.feedthechildren.org

LET YOUR EDUCATION SHINE THROUGH

Letter Twenty

Dear Daughters & YBW:

In this letter, I want to encourage you to let your education shine through. It is amazing to me how one can come out of a four-year institution of higher learning and yet appear to be ignorant and unlearned. Daughters and YBW, here's how you can let your education shine through:

First, let your education shine through by **having a healthy fear of God.** Proverbs 1:7 says: *"The fear of the Lord is the beginning of knowledge: but fools despise wisdom and instruction."* An educated young black woman will fear God so much so that she will not get puffed up with the knowledge she has. She realizes that without God, she could not have become an educated person.

Second, let your education shine through by **walking in humility.** Do not think that because you have some education, you know everything there is to know. There is a whole lot more that you will learn in life. The Bible tells us in I Corinthians 8:1 that *"Knowledge puffeth up, but charity edifieth."*

Third, let your education shine through in **your behavior and dress.** YBW, know how to act and dress appropriately in any given situation.

105

Fourth, let your education shine through **in your speech.** Do not come out of college sounding ignorant. Know what to say, when to say it, and how to say it. We are told in Proverbs 15:2 that: ***"The tongue of the wise useth knowledge aright: but the mouth of fools poureth out foolishness."***

Fifth, let your education shine through in **your writing.** Learn how to communicate well on paper.

Sixth, let your education shine through by **using the knowledge that you gain for good purposes.** Help others and give some of your time to worthy causes.

Seventh, let your education shine through by **thinking for yourself.** Do not let other people think for you. Size up what every person says to you by God's Word. Listening to other people who are not of God, can lead you away from God and cause you to mess up the rest of your life.

Daughters and YBW, let your education shine through and you will be the better for it.

Yours for Letting Your Education Shine,

P.T.:

♦ *"Those who travel the high road of humility are not troubled by heavy traffic."*

—*Alan K. Simpson*

♦ "From the first, I made my learning, what little it was, useful every way I could."

—Mary McLeod Bethune

BIBLE GEM: "Wise men lay up knowledge; but the mouth of the foolish is near destruction."

—Proverbs 10:14

TALK TO GOD: Dear Jesus, Help me to let my education show. Help me not to get puffed up or proud with the knowledge You have allowed me to gain. I thank You for the education that You have given to me. In Jesus Christ's name. Amen.

BOOK: Humility: True Greatness, by C.J. Mahaney

CHECK IT OUT: www.christianwomentoday.com

ABOVE ALL, GET WISDOM AND UNDERSTANDING

Letter Twenty-One

Dear Daughters & YBW:

Along with getting a good education, let me encourage you to get wisdom and understanding as well. Education will tell you *how* to do something, but wisdom will tell you *why* you should do something. King Solomon, the wisest man who ever lived, said in Proverbs 4:7 that *"Wisdom is the principal thing; therefore get wisdom: and with all thy getting get understanding."*

You ask, how can I obtain wisdom and understanding? There is only one way to get wisdom and that is simply to

ASK GOD FOR IT!

The Bible says in James 1:5, *"If any of you lack wisdom, let him ask of God, that giveth to all men liberally, and upbraideth not; and it shall be given him."*

Wisdom cannot be taught. Wisdom cannot be bought. It cannot be borrowed or extracted from others. Wisdom can only come from God, and if you have faith enough to ask Him, He has the grace enough to give it to you.

The glorious wisdom that God gives will help you to see so many things that you wouldn't see otherwise. Wisdom gives you a great advantage in life. Using wisdom can save you a lot of time and trouble in life. Again, let me say here, daughters, I believe many of the painful and devastating things so many young black women go through in our society today can be prevented in the first place, and having wisdom and understanding from God will help you to avoid these pitfalls. By the way, some of those pitfalls take a long time to overcome, so it's best not to fall into them in the first place.

I strongly encourage you to pray and ask God daily for wisdom and understanding to guide you through this life successfully.

With Wisdom and Love,

P.T.:

♦ *"To know the will of God is the highest of all wisdom."*
—*Billy Graham*

♦ *"Wisdom is the daughter of experience."*
—*Leonardo Da Vinci*

♦ *"We can be knowledgeable with other men's knowledge, but we cannot be wise with other men's wisdom."*
—*Michel de Montaigne*

BIBLE GEM: "For wisdom is better than rubies; and all the things that may be desired are not to be compared to it."
—*Proverbs 8:11*

TALK TO GOD: Dear God, I thank You for all of the education that You have allowed me to receive from my teachers, but Lord I pray that You would give me wisdom and understanding above everything else. Help me to use it for Your glory in all I have to do in my life. In Jesus Christ's Holy Name. Amen.

BOOK: Daily Wisdom for Women, by Carol L. Fitzpatrick

CHECK IT OUT: www.joycemeyer.org

ON YOUR LIFE — AS A YOUNG BLACK WOMAN

BEWARE OF THE DAWGS

Dear Daughters & **YBW**:

I trust that you are enjoying the life that God has given you.

In this letter, I want to lovingly warn you to beware of the dawgs. (In case you do not know what a dawg is, a dawg is a man who heartlessly plots to take advantage of women sexually with no intentions on marrying them. The connection between the man and the dog is this — have you ever seen a dog go down the church aisle and get married? The answer is "no." Dogs normally have sex with any dog they can have sex with, thus the term "dawg.") Interestingly enough, there is a verse in the Bible that actually says:

"Beware of dogs"
—Philippians 3:2

However, I think that they were talking about another kind of dog altogether. Notice that I spelled "dawg" differently because he is different — very different. Notice a few things about the dawg that I am talking about:

The Psychological Make-Up of the Dawg

The dawg can be developed out of any combination of family situations. He can come out of a home with a single parent, or with both parents, but he will almost always come out of a home situation where the mother was dominant and he was

115

pretty much left to himself. The dawg normally does not have the warmest relationship with his parents, particularly with his mother, probably because he feels she was not there for him while he was growing up; or because he saw her with other men besides his father; or perhaps he saw his mother disrespect and dishonor his father verbally and otherwise. Consequently, they somehow get a mentality that women are nothing but "B's" and "W's" to be conquered, subdued, taken advantage of, and sometimes abused.

The second part of the psychological make-up of a dawg is that no matter how cordial and handsome the dawg is, he is absolutely heartless. I am convinced that because of the childhood of the dawg, the young man who is classified as a dawg has no heart whatsoever. No matter what he says or what he does, he is almost incapable of loving a woman the way she should be loved and treating a woman the way she should be treated. You really need to understand this as a young woman because this kind of guy will chew you up and spit you out every time because he has no heart. Young men who are left to themselves while growing up turn out having no heart. Psychologists call this type of person a sociopath. We at the church call him a devil. He will have no remorse whatsoever about the pain he causes you, and in some cases, he won't even know he caused you any pain. This leads me to my next point about the dawg.

The Nature of the Dawg

Even though the dawg is heartless, largely because of his background, this does not mean he can't "put on the dog." The nature of the dawg, like the devil, is very deceptive. He looks good on the outside, but on the inside he is full of deceit

116

and corruption. The Bible says they will *"come to you in sheep's clothing, but inwardly they are ravening wolves"* (Matthew 7:15). His name might be "Angel," but he is a devil on the inside.

It is the nature of the dawg to feel as though, if given enough time to operate, he can get to any woman that he wants. It doesn't matter to him whether the woman is single or married. He is very confident that if he can get the woman alone, with enough time, he can deceive her into giving him what he wants — which in most cases is sex.

The Modus Operandi of the Dawg

You need to know how the dawg operates so that you can protect yourself from the dawg.

Now, the first thing the dawg knows is that *you have some weaknesses.* In other words, he will probe for a weakness, a dark spot in your own life. You see, the dawg is convinced that there is some evil in you too.

The second thing that the dawg wants to work on is *eye contact,* for the dawg feels that if he can make good eye contact with you, he is fifty percent toward his goal. Now, mind you, the dawg does not care who you are, or who you are with, be it your boyfriend, husband, or parents. He truly believes in his mind that if he can get some good eye contact with you, he can get you. Sister, don't let anybody fool you; there is power in the eyes. Whatever you do, DON'T GIVE HIM YOUR EYES IF YOU DON'T WANT HIM TO GET YOU.

Now, if he is successful at these two points, the dawg begins to work *his psychological magic.* For example, at school or at work, he will come by your desk and just tap it and wave with a smile. At this point, he won't say anything; he will just wave and smile. He'll do this for several weeks. Now you won't know what is going on, but he is working on you. And you will begin thinking, "Oh, he's just such a nice guy." That is exactly what he wants you to think. At that point, the dawg will begin to pour on his charm, and what he wants you to think is that he is expressing "feelings of love" toward you. Now when the dawg begins to express some "feelings of love" toward you, don't be deceived. When he begins to say that he loves you, watch out! The dawg is lying and telling you the truth at the same time. Oh! He loves you. He loves the shape of your body, he loves the softness of your skin, he loves the sound of your voice, and he loves the way you smell. Yes, he loves you alright. He loves what you can do for him, and how you can make him feel.

In closing, how do so many young women get taken by dawgs, and why are good girls attracted to bad boys, or dawgs?

> First, many of us wrongly think that good girls or church-going girls are all good, and that they don't have any evil in them. I hate to be the one to tell you, but that is simply not the case. Unfortunately, what oftentimes draws the good church girl to the bad boy is the bad in the good church girl, which the Bible calls the flesh.

> Second, young women are attracted to masculinity, and oftentimes, the good church boy appears so weak

and effeminate that the good church girl is turned off by that, and associates masculinity with the "bad boyness" of the dawg.

Third, no one takes the time to teach the good church girl how to discern when she is dealing with a dawg, and how to protect herself from the dawg.

Fourth, the love of the forbidden. Unfortunately, because of our sinful nature, we all have an attraction oftentimes to that which is mysterious, dark, evil, and forbidden. The dawg is all of that and more.

Fifth, sometimes, some young women don't want to be protected from the dawg, and therefore, they do not take heed to the warning signs. This letter is a huge warning sign to you. You can avoid much pain and heartache if you take heed to it.

Daughters and YBW, thousands upon thousands of young black women have been deceived by dawgs, and thus bitten by dawgs. The sad thing about the bite of these dawgs is that the scars seldom go away. Most times, there is a permanent scar that affects her and therefore her relationships for the rest of her life. As I said earlier, this book is about prevention; don't let this happen to you.

BEWARE OF THE DAWGS!

Papa

P.T.:

Daughters and YBW, I am ashamed to tell you that one of the reasons why I know so much about the dawg is because I was once a dawg myself. So it would behoove you to listen to what I have to say. Below, I will tell you how to avoid being bitten by the dawgs.

How to Control the Dawgs

1. Never give them your eyes.

2. Do not get sucked in by the dawgs' good looks and charm. In the words of Rev. James T. Meeks of Chicago, "Watch out for Pretty Tony!" because his bite can be devastating.

3. Never put yourself in a compromising position with a dawg. In other words, do not get in a car alone with a dawg, don't go to the dawg's house, and don't let the dawg come over to your house, because the dawg always bites.

4. Don't pet the dawg. (In other words, don't touch the dawg, and don't let the dawg touch you.) Remember the verse in I Corinthians 7:1 that says, "It is good for a man not to touch a woman."

5. Let your father, your pastor, or an older brother meet the young dawg. I assure you they will be able to discern what he is about in 30 seconds or less. This suggestion alone, if heeded, can save you a lifetime of heartache and pain. (Notice, I did not mention your mother in this list because, sad to say, many mothers can't pick up on the dawg like a man can.)

6. Make a commitment to God that the first man you kiss and have sex with will be your husband

120

— no exceptions. Wear your chastity ring every day, and don't just wear it for show.

NEVER HAVE SEX BEFORE MARRIAGE UNDER ANY CIRCUMSTANCES!

BIBLE GEM: "Be sober, be vigilant; because your adversary the devil, as a roaring lion, walketh about, seeking whom he may devour."

—1 Peter 5:8

TALK TO GOD: Dear Lord, Help me to beware of evil men. Help me to stay a virgin until You provide me a husband. But in the meanwhile, Lord, please protect me and give me Your wisdom and guidance. I thank You for loving me. In Jesus Christ's name. Amen.

BOOK: *He Loves Me, He Loves Me Not: What Every Woman Needs to Know About Unconditional Love, but Is Afraid to Feel*, by Paula White

BEWARE OF THE DAWGS II
(Who Let the Dawgs Out?)

Letter Twenty-Three

Dear Daughters & YBW:

After writing my last letter to you, I got into bed and was about to go to sleep, when the idea came to my mind that I should write you and tell you specifically the different kinds of dawgs of which you should be aware. Here they are:

Collie Dawg: I don't know about you, but when I think about a Collie dog, I think about the old television show *Lassie*. Now, *Lassie* might be before your time. But all Collies, like Lassie, are considered "smart" dogs. So you have to watch out for the Collie dawg because he is a smart dawg. This dawg is a master of psychology. He plans. He plots. He thinks. The Collie plays games with your mind. He is a mind-manipulator. He plays games with you, like taking you out and showing you the time of your life, and then leaves you panting for more. Then you won't hear from him for a couple of weeks because he is trying to mess with your mind. Watch out for the Collie Dawg.

Chow-Chow Dawg: This dawg hooks women because he is so pretty. Have you ever seen a Chow-Chow? It's a beautiful dog, isn't it? I remember when I was a youngster, there was a man in town (I won't tell you his name; I'll just call him D.B.). The women were so crazy about him because he was so pretty. You know the type — light skin, curly "good" hair, fine build. But the women soon found out that he was just another dawg — albeit a pretty dawg. D.B. was famous for one thing in our little city, and that was having babies all over town. The problem with the Chow-Chow dawg is that he may be pretty, but oftentimes, he does not want to take responsibility for his actions. The pretty dawg wants you to take care of him instead of him taking care of you. Remember, watch out for "Pretty Tony."

Great Dane Dawg: Be careful and watch out for the Great Dane dawg. He likes to hook unsuspecting women through his sexual prowess. He's the kind that brags about his abilities. This causes some women to be curious like Eve was, and like a dumb fish, they get hooked, and this dawg reels them in, and devours them.

Poodle Dawg: Watch out for the Poodle dawg! Now this is a dangerous dawg because he's got some sugar in his tank. This is the effeminate dawg. He prides himself on having a male side and a female side. He goes both ways. He hooks women by being able to relate to them. He knows how to get close to you like one of your girlfriends. This is how so many women get fooled, and sadly, get AIDS because behind his sweet personality is a dawg in the truest sense. This dawg can be on the "down-low," therefore making him a "low-down" dawg. Watch out, I tell you! **Warning: All dawgs listed in this list can give you a venereal disease, including AIDS.**

Seeing Eye Dawg: Now the Seeing Eye dawg is the go everywhere dawg. You will even find this dawg in church — which makes him a very dangerous dawg indeed. He can be saved or lost (yes, there are some "saved" brothers who walk in the dawg from time to time). Women trust him

124

because he is in the church, and that is how he gets over on them. This dawg is very sneaky, so keep your eyes open.

Special Warning: Daughters and YBW, I hate to have to share this with you, but I would encourage you to never seek counseling with a pastor or a male leader in the church alone. Always take someone with you, such as, an older lady of the church or even the pastor's wife. And never meet with a pastor or any church leader behind closed doors under any circumstances; because, sad to say, there are some Seeing Eye dawgs in the pulpit.

Rottweiler Dawg: Now the Rottweiler dawg likes to fight. If things don't go the way he wants them to go, he wants to fight you. He just can't get angry, say a few words, and walk away. He's got to give you a black eye, and send you to the hospital. Strangely enough, though, he gets his share of women. I strongly urge you to stay away from this dawg because this dawg is not only known to bite; he's known to kill as well.

Pit Bull Dawg: Now the Pit Bull dawg is crazy. He may be built fine, but this is a crazy dawg. He's schizophrenic. This dawg may be nice one day, and then mean as the devil the next. He hooks women by his unpredictability and craziness. Some women are attracted to him because they see him as exciting, thrilling, and a man that offers them a big challenge to tame him. Don't get sucked in by this crazy dawg.

Bull Dawg: The Bull dawg is stubborn. You can't tell the Bull dawg anything because he is bull-headed. He won't go to college, and he won't go to church because he thinks he already knows everything. He always has something to say, but never wants to listen to anybody. You don't want to get entangled with this dawg because this dawg is a foolish dawg that will lead you to nowhere fast.

Hound Dawg: Do you remember the song "You Ain't Nothing But a Hound Dog," by Elvis Presley? Well, that is what you have here. The Hound dawg is a lazy dawg. He expects you to take care of him. Normally, he can't keep a job, and he doesn't pay what few bills he does have on time. He never has any money to give to you, but he always has his hand out behind his back for some money from you. If you are not careful, the Hound dawg will have you taking care of him. Let a sleeping dawg lie.

Chihuahua Dawg: The Chihuahua dawg is normally a little man with a big mouth. He has a Napoleanic complex. He is insecure, and his bark is bigger than his bite. He knows how to get to some women with his ability to rap. He talks a big game, but he ain't about nothing. These dawgs can't back up what they talk about. All this dawg ends up doing is disappointing you. Don't waste your time.

Alaskan Huskie Dawg: Now, the Alaskan Huskie is a hard-working dawg. This dawg hooks women because he always has some money. He drives a nice car that he keeps immaculate. He has a nice house. He is known to keep two or three jobs. Well, at least he works, but a dawg is a dawg is a dawg. You have to watch this dawg because he will hook you with what he has, but he is so stingy that he won't share it with you unless you pay up what you have to offer, which is normally sex. Beware of this dawg.

The Show Dawg: Now the Show dawg is a good-for-nothing dawg. He is only good for show. This is the empty-hand and empty-pocket dawg who looks good on your arm when you go to important events. This dawg looks good and smells good, but he is of no use to you at all. He can't do anything without you. You don't want this kind of dawg. He will drag you down, and, as they say, "You can do bad all by yourself."

German Shepherd Dawg: You can depend on the German Shepherd dawg for the most part. He is basically a good dawg, but when he turns on you, you are through. You see, the German Shepherd will appeal to you because of his faithfulness and dependability, but if you cross him, you are in trouble. The problem is that you will never know when the line is crossed.

Irish Setter Dawg: Be very careful with the Irish Setter dawg because he is another lazy dawg — only he will run right for a little while giving you the appearance that he's looking for a job, but then he will sit down on you, and you will be taking care of him. (Never take care of a man.) This is the dawg who likes to sit in your house all day with the remote control watching television while you are at work. Don't let the Irish Setter sit down on you.

Pointer Dawg: This dawg likes to point at others. This dawg has a critical spirit. He loves to point at everybody else's faults but his own. Watch this dawg, because he starts out well, and he seems as though he is helpful, but really he is out to break you down, and make you think that you are crazy, like he is some psychiatrist or something.

Daughters and YBW, there are many other dawgs out there, so watch carefully. I do not have the time or space to tell you about each of them specifically. I wish I did. However, if it walks like a dawg, if it smells like a dawg, and if it looks like a dawg, IT IS A DAWG. RUN!

Beware of the Dawgs!

Papa

P.T.:

♦ "God loves His girls."

—T.D. Jakes

BIBLE GEM: "Beware of dogs, beware of evil workers, beware of the concision."

—Philippians 3:2

TALK TO GOD: Holy Father God, I pray that You would help me to watch out for men who don't mean me any good. Protect me and give me wisdom and discernment in this area of my life. In Jesus Christ's holy name. Amen.

BOOK: *Promises from God for Single Women,* by T.D. Jakes

CHECK IT OUT: www.sbcoc.org (Pastor James Meeks has a sermon that deals with some other dawgs of which you need to be aware. Order the tape or CD from the aforementioned website.)

ON NOT BEING A SILLY-MINDED WOMAN

Letter Twenty-Four

Dear Daughters & YBW:

Notice what Paul says in II Timothy 3:6: *"For of this sort are they which creep into houses, and lead captive <u>silly women</u> laden with sins, led away with divers lusts."*

I know that I am going to make some folks angry by suggesting that there are some silly-minded women in the world. The fact of the matter, however, is that there are silly-minded women in this world, and my purpose in writing this letter to you is to encourage you not to be one of them.

Now, what do I mean when I use the term "silly-minded" women? I know that it is painful to talk about, but if you'll be honest, you'll probably admit to knowing some silly-minded women. A silly-minded woman is a woman who is not known to be a thinker. She is a woman who is considered easy. Like Eve, she is easily deceived by the devil. She is easily tricked by cunning men. She is a woman who is not guided by absolutes, moral principles, or facts; rather, she is guided by her emotions and feelings only. Therefore, periodically, throughout her life, she gets herself into terrible messes with God, with men, with people on her job, and even with her children. She is a woman who is not characterized by prayer, thoughtfulness, positive action, soberness, and vigilance. She doesn't keep her guard up in life. Therefore, she is constantly bombarded by people and things that keep her from fulfilling

God's purpose for her life. Obviously, the powerful verse found in I Peter 5:8 is not on her mind: ***"Be sober, be vigilant, because your adversary the devil, as a roaring lion, walketh about, seeking whom he may devour."***

Here are some further characteristics of a silly-minded woman:

1. **She does not know her purpose in life.** Therefore, she meanders through life not accomplishing anything worthwhile.

2. **She does not know her passion in life.** I am forever amazed at women, who even at the age of thirty-five, don't know what their interests are, and don't know what they like to do. They end up wasting half of their lives.

3. **She does not know what her gifts are.** At some point, it should dawn on you the gifts and talents of which God has endowed you. For example, if God has given you the ability to sing, then at some point you should realize that this is your gift to the world, and you should begin to use it to be a blessing to others. On the other hand, if your gift is not singing, at some point, you should realize that as well and stop irritating people. A woman who does not know her gift ends up wasting the talent with which God has blessed her.

4. **She does not have clear direction in her life.** In other words, her life is not going forward in a straight line. She has no goals, and if she does, she allows herself to get off track. For example, she may say, "I'm going

back to college to finish my degree." Then while she is in college, moving forward with her life, she'll meet Tyrone, and before you know it, she's pregnant and her life is off track again.

5. **She is disorganized.** She does not keep her house clean, she can never find important papers, she doesn't have proof of insurance, and her car is a mess. Therefore, she wastes time looking for things.

6. **She does not have a plan for the next day.** Therefore, she is always shocked and surprised at things that happen to her. She is reactive instead of proactive. She does not make things happen; things constantly happen to her.

7. **She does not live by lists.** She does not realize the value of written lists, and that people who accomplish things in life operate from them. Therefore, her life is circular instead of straight forward.

8. **She is rebellious and stubborn, and does not listen to sound counsel.** The Bible says, *"A foolish woman is clamorous: she is simple, and knoweth nothing"* (Proverbs 9:13). The consequence is she ends up ruining her life and wasting other people's time.

9. **She is a liar.** She tries to lie her way out of the messes she gets herself in, thus putting herself in more bondage, not realizing that only the truth can set her free.

10. **She does not keep her mind occupied with positive and good things**. For example, she feeds on foolish

novels and television shows, and when she has to wait in a doctor's office, or wait for some other kind of appointment, she would rather look around at other people than read a book, thus wasting valuable time.

11. **If she somehow gets married, instead of building her family and household up, she tears it down** with her bad attitude, lying, rebelliousness, etc. The Bible refers to this when it says: ***"Every wise woman buildeth her house: but the foolish plucketh it down with her hands"*** (Proverbs 14:1).

Sisters, I can go further, but time and space would fail me. Here's how you can avoid being a silly-minded woman, and be a strong-minded, virtuous woman instead:

First, **be a woman of prayer**. Pray about every little thing. The woman who prays allows God to direct her life. ***"In all thy ways acknowledge Him, and He shall direct thy paths"*** (Proverbs 3:6). Praying throughout the day will help you to be sober-minded and vigilant at all times. ***"Pray without ceasing"*** (I Thessalonians 5:17).

Second, **read and meditate on God's Word**. Allow God's Word to speak to your heart and mind, and to guide you throughout the day. Also, let the Word of God remind you of your duties as a Christian.

Third, **go through each day with a purpose**. Each day you need to know what God wants you to do. Make sure that everything you do is centered around the purpose that God has for you in your life. Even taking time for a little rest and relaxation is a part of God's purpose for your life.

Fourth, **you must think for yourself**. If the Holy Spirit and your conscience tells you that something is wrong, then it is wrong. Don't be swayed by every wind of doctrine that enters the world. Don't allow yourself to be blown away by every man who comes your way, and make sure that all of your decisions are based on the Holy Spirit's guidance and the eternal Word of God.

Fifth, **stay busy**. Keep moving. Once you finish one task or goal, have another one ready to do. You know the old saying, "An idle mind is the devil's playground." Just because it is an old saying does not mean it is not true. Wherever you go, always have something with you on which to work. If you don't want every Tom, Dick, and Harry trying to talk with you throughout the day, you must be a woman who looks like she is on the go, like she is on a mission, like she has things to do, people to see, and places to go. The strong-minded woman — the virtuous woman — is industrious. Notice what the Bible says about the virtuous woman in Proverbs 31:13: *"She seeketh wool, and flax, and worketh willingly with her hands."*

Sixth, **be a woman who cares for other people, and who tries to meet the needs of suffering humanity**. Having a caring heart for other people will keep you busy all by itself. The Bible says of the virtuous woman: *"She stretcheth out her hand to the poor; yea, she reacheth forth her hands to the needy"* (Proverbs 31:20).

Seventh, **keep your mind occupied with positive things**. The Bible says in Philippians 4:8: *"Finally, brethren, whatsoever things are true, whatsoever things are honest, whatsoever things are just, whatsoever things are pure,* *whatsoever things are lovely, whatsoever things are of good report; if there be any virtue, and if there be any praise, think on these things."*

In closing, I should mention the benefits of being a strong, tough-minded woman, for they are numerous:

1. You can laugh at the devil because he can't touch you.

2. You can laugh at dawggish men who mean you no good. No man will be able to tell his buddies that he had you, and that you ain't about nothing.

3. You can get many wonderful things accomplished with your life before the age of twenty-four: things like getting your doctorate degree, starting a business, writing your first novel or non-fiction book, buying your first house, buying the car of your dreams, reading all of the classics, and the list could go on and on.

4. You can be a blessing to your parents instead of a burden.

5. You can save a whole lot of time and money.

6. You can travel around the world on missionary trips.

7. Along with your other degree, you can get a seminary degree to serve more effectively in your church.

8. You will never get hurt romantically by getting tied up with a man who God did not choose to be your husband in the first place. As you know, this can take up to three years, and sometimes even a life time to get over. What a colossal

waste of valuable time.

9. You can avoid many aggravating day-to-day problems and troubles by being organized and having all your paperwork in order, including proof of insurance.

10. You can avoid the devastating consequences of lying. Sister, if people cannot trust you and your word, your life is doomed. The sad thing about it is that you won't even know it because your employers and so-called friends won't have the guts to check you on your lying. They will just silently take note of it, tell others about it, and never trust you again.

Daughters and YBW, please forgive me for this rather long-winded letter. I just don't want you to be a silly-minded woman; rather, I want you to be a strong, tough-minded woman, who makes things happen in her life, instead of letting things happen to her.

Be Strong,

Papa

P.T.:

♦ *"I have learned over the years that when one's mind is made up, this diminishes fear; knowing what must be done does away with fear."*
—*Rosa Parks*

♦ *"In matters of style, swim with the current; in matters of principle, stand like a rock."*
—*Thomas Jefferson*

BIBLE GEM: "*Therefore, my beloved brethren, be ye stedfast, unmoveable, always abounding in the work of the Lord, forasmuch as ye know that your labour is not in vain in the Lord.*"

—I Corinthians 15:58

TALK TO GOD: Dear God, Please help me to be a strong-minded woman for You, and help me not to fall for every wind of doctrine that may come along. In Jesus Christ's powerful name. Amen.

BOOK: Battlefield of the Mind: Winning the Battle in Your Mind, by Joyce Meyer

CHECK IT OUT: www.joycemeyer.org

ON STAYING A VIRGIN UNTIL YOU ARE MARRIED

Letter Twenty-Five

Dear Daughters & YBW:

You cannot lose by remaining a virgin until you are happily married to that special someone. Virgins always WIN!

It is not fair, but in the minds of most men, when a girl loses her virginity, she loses a whole lot. In their minds, her value goes down; but strangely, when a man loses his virginity, his stock goes up, not only in the minds of the fellows, but also in the minds of the women as well. This may not be fair, but oftentimes it is true.

Most men have real problems in their heads if their woman has been with another man sexually. You may call it insecurity, or whatever, but it is a reality. I believe it stems from the fact that God is a jealous God, and God made man in His image; thus man has some good jealousy in him. In my own case, I don't know where it came from, but even though I was not a virgin, I knew I couldn't marry a woman who was not a virgin. When God showed me I needed to get married, I literally traveled the world to find a Christian woman who was a virgin. Out of the nine women who I had dated over the course of two years, only one was able to say she was a virgin — Daughters, I married that woman, and she is your mother. You can call that whatever you want; you can call it unfair, you can call it insecurity, you can call it out-of-control jealousy, but the truth of the matter is, like most men, I just did not want to have in my mind that what my wife is doing with me now, sexually, she had done with another man. Now today, most men will not have the guts to tell you what I just told you because it is not cool for a man to have jealousy for his wife. Even though it is not cool in our society today, any man who loves his wife, or wife to be, will be jealous over her. And you should know this, YBW, since, deep down, every woman wants her husband to have some jealousy for her as proof of his love, as long as it is not crazy jealousy.

As I indicated earlier, many men will not be as bold as I was, and actually ask the young woman if she is a virgin. Today that is not cool. But trust me, when he is thinking about marriage, that is at the forefront of his mind. Strangely, more than the woman, the man wants to know where you have been, who you have been with, and what you did. Now, if he does not love you and care for you, and he just wants to use you for sex, then he will not care whether you are a virgin or not. Remember, as I said earlier, most men today do not have the guts to ask a young lady what is really on his mind. But just because he is afraid to ask does not mean it is not on his mind. Stay a virgin until you are married, so that this will never be an issue with you and your future husband because this will indeed come up. If the young man does not have the guts to ask you before marriage, when the heat is on in the marriage, it is going to come up. While you and your husband are out at the mall or at the grocery store, he's going to have a hard time dealing with meeting one of your old boyfriends with whom he knows you have had sex.

Sister, the world will tell you differently. It will tell you that it is okay to try other men out before you settle down. However, God's Word is true and is the best way for you to

138

go. Notice the following verses:

"Flee fornication. Every sin that a man doeth is without the body; but he that committeth fornication sinneth against his own body."

—I Corinthians 6:18

"Now concerning the things whereof ye wrote unto me: It is good for a man not to touch a woman. Nevertheless, to avoid fornication, let every man have his own wife, and let every woman have her own husband."

—I Corinthians 7:1 & 2

Here are four reasons why you ought not to have sex before marriage:

1. It will cost you more than it will cost him. I know it's not fair, but it is true. It's kind of like the story of the chicken and the pig. The chicken came to the pig and said, "Let's provide a good breakfast for Farmer John by giving him some good old bacon and eggs. You can provide the bacon, and I can provide the eggs." The pig said, "That sounds good. However, yours is just a donation; mine is a complete sacrifice." In this story, you, young lady, are the pig.

2. It will break your fellowship with God and steal your joy, peace, and moral authority. You don't want that.

3. You can get pregnant. He will probably go on to marry somebody else, and go on with the rest of

his life. You will have a constant reminder of your moral failure, and remember: the child is never illegitimate — the parents are. The child is a gift from God.

4. It can cause you untold heartache and pain throughout your life.

How to avoid having sex before marriage:

1. Never put yourself in a compromising position.

2. Never send the wrong signal to the opposite sex.

3. Make up your mind what you are going to do before the temptation comes, and as sure as I am black and my last name is Whyte, the temptation is going to come.

4. Never travel or go places alone. Always go with your sisters, or your girlfriends — better yet, go with your big brother.

5. Stay with your parents until you get married, and obey the rules of their house. For example, in such a situation, Tyrone can't stay until 11:00 at night, and you can't stay at Tyrone's house until 11:00 at night. Never disrespect your parents, no matter how old you are.

Fly Virgin,

P.T.:

♦ *"You are built not to shrink down to less but to blossom into more."*

—*Oprah Winfrey*

♦ *"A life of peace, purity, and refinement leads to a calm and untroubled old age."*

—*Cicero*

♦ *"It is well to think well; it is divine to act well."*

—*Horace Mann*

♦ *"I married the first man I ever kissed."*

—*Barbara Bush*

♦ *"Freedom is not the right to do as you please, but the liberty to do as you ought."*

—*Selected*

BIBLE GEM: **"What? know ye not that your body is the temple of the Holy Ghost which is in you, which ye have of God, and ye are not your own? For ye are bought with a price: therefore glorify God in your body, and in your spirit, which are God's."**

—*1 Corinthians 6:19 & 20*

TALK TO GOD: *Holy Father, I pray that You would help me to be the woman that You want me to be. Help me to remain a virgin and to abstain from all sexual activities before marriage. Thank You for Your love and help. In Jesus Christ's precious name. Amen.*

BOOK: *The Diva Principle,* by Michelle McKinney Hammond

CHECK IT OUT: www.ceeceemichaela.com

IF YOU DESIRE TO GET MARRIED, HERE IS HOW TO GET A GOOD MAN

Letter Twenty-Six

Dear Daughters & YBW:

As I have said to you many times, if I were a woman, I wouldn't be bothered with getting married. I would get my education, pursue my purpose in life, do missionary work, travel, and just have myself a grand old time. However, I am not a woman. What women see in men, I have no clue, but that is how God has wired us. He made men to be attracted to women, and women to be attracted to men. (Even though today, we have many men and women who are getting it all twisted up — if you know what I mean.)

Be that as it may, if you want to get married to a great man, a man who will love the Lord and who will love you, here is what you need to do:

1. **Start praying to God now for the husband He wants you to have.** God still answers prayer. Jesus Christ said in Matthew 7:7: *"Ask, and it shall be given you; seek, and ye shall find; knock, and it shall be opened unto you."* Daughters, from the time your mother, Meriqua, was a little girl, she prayed for and desired a preacher as a husband, and that is what she got. (Only she did not specify what kind of preacher. You better be specific.)

143

2. **If you want a good man, you must be a good woman.** What is a good woman? Well, in short, a good woman is:

    a. A woman who is trustworthy. She tells the truth, the whole truth, and nothing but the truth every time. According to the Scriptures about the virtuous woman, it says that *"The heart of her husband doth safely trust in her, so that he shall have no need of spoil."*

    b. A woman who knows how to show respect for her man. She has the wisdom to let the man be a man, and she never does anything to embarrass him, at home, or elsewhere. She knows that the main thing a man wants, even above love itself, is respect. The Bible says in Ephesians 5:33: *"And the wife see that she reverence her husband."*

    c. A good woman knows that she must take care of her husband, her children, and her home before she tries to take care of other people's business. She is willing to let the job go if it's taking away from domestic tranquility. Notice what the Bible says in Proverbs 7:11 about the bad woman: *"She is loud and stubborn; her feet abide not in her house."*

3. **Keep yourself pure at all costs.** (Please see Letter 25 entitled "On Staying a Virgin until You Get Married.") Be pure in your spirit, be pure in your mind, be pure in your heart, and be pure in your body. It is amazing how God makes that pureness to shine through. Have you ever seen a young woman, say

around twenty-two, but when you get up close to her, she looks like she is forty-two? Well, that comes from living a fast, impure life. You can't hide purity, and you can't hide impurity either.

4. **Don't look for a man.** Whatever you do, do not look for a man. When God wants you to get married, He will bring the man to you. Do you remember the stories of Rachel and Rebekah in the Bible, and how God miraculously blessed them with two great men as their husbands? God actually brought their husbands to them; they did not go looking for their husbands. We have absolutely too many young women today on the hunt for good men. The problem with that is if you get a good man, and God is not in it, there will be hell to pay. One of the most pitiful sights in America is a desperate black woman.

5. **Plan your life to be with a man, and plan your life to be without a man.** I say this because I do not want you to feel badly about yourself if you don't get married. The truth of the matter is that there are not that many good black men to choose from, and that is no fault of God's or yours. It is the fault of the choices that many young black men have made. We have too many young black men in jail; we have too many young black men who are homosexuals; and we have too many young black men who won't finish high school and attend college, and therefore, can't support a family if they had one.

6. **Trust the Lord!** I am afraid, that we have many young women today who go to church on Sunday, and say that they trust in the Lord, but they really don't. They go right on out of the church and try to make things happen themselves.

7. **If you do the right thing, you will be in the right place, at the right time.** Always walk in the will of God, and He'll put you in the right place at the right time. God's Word says in Psalm 37:4: ***Delight thyself also in the Lord; and he shall give thee the desires of thine heart."***

These are just some thoughts that will help you get the man that God wants you to have.

With Lots of Love,

Papa

P.T.:

♦ *"Do not open your heart to every man, but discuss your affairs with one who is wise and who fears God."*

—Thomas à Kempis

BIBLE GEM: "Many waters cannot quench love, neither can the floods drown it: if a man would give all the substance of his house for love, it would utterly be contemned."

—Song of Solomon 8:7

146

TALK TO GOD: Holy Father, I pray that if it is Your will, that You would send me the husband that You want me to have. I pray that in the meantime, You would make me into the godly, virtuous, and caring woman that You want me to be. Prepare my future husband for me and me for him, and I leave the rest of the details up to You. In Your Holy name. Amen.

BOOK: Jacob and Rachel: The Greatest Love Story, by *Helen Wood*

CHECK IT OUT: <u>www.michellehammond.com</u>

THE CASE FOR NEVER GETTING MARRIED

Letter Twenty-Seven

Dear Daughters & YBW:

"Now concerning the things whereof ye wrote unto me: It is good for a man not to touch a woman."
—I Corinthians 7:1

This is not going to sit well with many of my traditional friends, but as I mentioned before, if I were a young black woman in today's world, I wouldn't think much at all about getting married. But, alas, I am not a girl, so I really do not know what it is that drives a woman to a man.

Granted, there was a time when women were considered "old maids" if they were not married by a certain age, but that is not the case today. Does Condoleezza Rice look like an "old maid" to you? Now, this is just me; I have my questions and doubts about a young man who is 30 or 40 years of age who doesn't have a girlfriend, and who is not, and has never been married; but I don't give a second thought about a single woman of that age who has never been married. In fact, if she is maintaining herself with class, dignity, and ease, as it appears Condoleezza Rice is doing, I consider her wise, because if I were a woman, I wouldn't give these weak, irresponsible, and effeminate men of today the time of day.

Here is the case for never getting married:

1. The Bible makes it very clear that if one is able to contain himself or herself sexually, it is better to stay single. I Corinthians 7:8,9 says: *"I say therefore to the unmarried and widows, It is good for them if they abide even as I. But if they cannot contain, let them marry: for it is better to marry than to burn."*

2. If you stay single, you can do more for the Lord. I Corinthians 7:34 says: *"The unmarried woman careth for the things of the Lord, that she may be holy both in body and in spirit."*

3. If you stay single, you have the freedom to do more of what you like to do, whereas if you get married, you have to focus more on the needs of your family: *"She that is married careth for the things of the world, how she may please her husband"* (I Corinthians 7:34b).

In fact, **DON'T GET MARRIED IF YOU ARE NOT WILLING TO DO THE FOLLOWING:**

1. Get your pleasure, and fulfillment out of helping your husband, nurturing your children, and caring for others. Put your husband and children before yourself.

2. Submit to your husband's leadership. The Bible says in Ephesians 5:22: *"Wives, submit yourselves unto your own husbands, as unto the Lord."*

3. Obey your husband. Ephesians 5:24 says: *"Therefore as the church is subject unto Christ, so let the wives be to their own husbands in everything."*

4. Love your husband, and be willing to have sex with him as often as he wants to. The Bible says in I Corinthians 7:4: ***"The wife hath not power of her own body, but the husband: and likewise also the husband hath not power of his own body, but the wife."***

5. Love your children, and spend lots of time with them including changing nasty diapers.

6. Wait, perhaps, for years to get praised and rewarded for the sacrifices that you made. The Bible says in Proverbs 31:25 that, ***"She shall rejoice in time to come."***

You can get married or not get married — the choice is yours — but if I were a woman in this day and time, I would strongly consider,

Flying Solo,

Papa

P.T.:

♦ *"Marriage is like twirling a baton, turning handsprings, or eating with chopsticks; it looks so easy till you try it."*
—Helen Rowland

♦ *"The exercise that really changes your life is walking down the aisle."*
—Mary Ellen Pinkham

♦ "I wish someone would have told me that, just because I'm a girl, I don't have to get married."
—Marlo Thomas

♦ "We must stop trying to make things happen the way we want them to happen and get to the place where we want to please God more than ourselves."
—Joyce Meyer

♦ "Everything in our lives happens for a purpose and that purpose is to prepare us."
—Spencer W. Kimball

BIBLE GEM: "But she is happier if she so abide, after my judgment: and I think also that I have the Spirit of God."
—I Corinthians 7:40

TALK TO GOD: Holy Father, I pray that if it be in Your will for me to stay single and to serve You with everything that I have, I pray that You would give me the grace to do it. I know that You created marriage and that You also created those to wholly devote their time and attention to You. I leave Your plans for my life up to You. In Jesus Christ's precious name. Amen.

BOOK: Sassy, Single, and Satisfied: Secrets to Loving the Life You're Living, by Michelle McKinney Hammond

CHECK IT OUT: www.bfmmm.com

THE KIND OF MAN YOU SHOULD NOT MARRY

Letter Twenty-Eight

Dear Daughters & YBW:

As you know, there is much questioning, particularly in the church, about who can find a virtuous woman. An equally important question, one that is in the Bible as well but that is not mentioned much, is found in Proverbs 20:6: *"...A faithful man who can find?"*

In this day and time, the truth of the matter is that there are not many virtuous women, and there are not many faithful men either, and that leads me to the kind of man you should not marry:

- **Don't marry a man who is not a Christian**, a man who does not love God nor fear God. For if you marry a man who neither knows God or fears God, you and your marriage are in a world of trouble. The Word of God clearly states in II Corinthians 6:14: *"Be ye not unequally yoked together with unbelievers: for what fellowship hath righteousness with unrighteousness? and what communion hath light with darkness?"* You had better ask the question on that new book entitled, *He May Be Fine But Is He Saved?* If you violate the verse above, you will have hell to pay. Mark my words.

- **Don't marry a dawg** because dawgs have no heart (See Letters 22 & 23).

- **Don't marry an unfaithful man**. In other words, don't marry a man who is unfaithful to God, unfaithful to his church, and unfaithful to you. A faithful man is hard to find, but if God blesses you with one, you have a blessing indeed.

- **Don't marry a deadbeat**. Please don't marry a man who is lazy, who is listless, and who has no drive nor purpose in life. Marry a man who is about something, and who is going somewhere because if he is going somewhere, he'll take you with him. Marry a man with a dream and a vision.

- **Don't marry a wimp**. Don't marry a weak, effeminate man who cannot think and do independently of you. Why? Because within a few weeks you are going to get tired of doing his job and your job too. Frankly, you will get bored with him.

- **Don't marry a broke man**. Here's the rule you should follow — whether you choose to work or not, all household bills, including your car note, should be paid out of *his* money. Your check should not be depended upon to take care of the household.

And, by the way, don't bring the following young men home either:

- A young man with more gold in his mouth than he has in his pocket.

- A young man with his cap on backwards and an earring in his ear.
- A young man with no car.
- A young man that I have to help get a job.
- A young man with a low rider car that bounces up and down.
- A young man without a college degree.
- A young man who does not come from a good family.
- A young man with braids in his hair and his pants hanging off his behind.

You get my drift? These jokers won't make it in the Whyte House, so don't bring them here.

If you marry, marry a saved, strong, faithful man that you can respect, love, and on whom you can depend.

Marry Well,

Papa

P.T.:

♦ *"Even if marriages are made in Heaven, man has to be responsible for the maintenance."*
　　　　　　　　　　　　　　—Dr. James Dobson

♦ *"A successful marriage requires falling in love many times, always with the same person."*
　　　　　　　　　　　　　—Mignon McLaughlin

♦ *"More marriages might survive if the partners realized that sometimes the better comes after the worse."*　　　　　　　　　*—Doug Larson*

BIBLE GEM: "And now abideth faith, hope, charity, these three; but the greatest of these is charity."
—I Corinthians 13:13

TALK TO GOD: Holy Father, Please protect me from marrying the wrong man. If it is Your will for me to get married, please bless me with the man that You want me to have. In Jesus Christ's name I pray. Amen.

BOOK: The Five Love Languages, by Gary Chapman

CHECK IT OUT: www.family.org

HOW TO THINK LIKE A MAN YET BE ALL WOMAN

Letter Twenty-Nine

Dear Daughters & YBW:

Years ago, long before you were born, James Brown sang a song entitled *It's A Man's World*. Thankfully, it is not a man's world. Rather, it is God's world, and men, women, and children have their part to play in it. Women are just as important as men, but they do have their role to play in God's world. James Brown was a little bit off, but not too far off.

Contrary to what the feminists of our society would tell you, God did put men on earth to be leaders, and to fulfill their role as protectors and providers. The women that men like to be around the most are those dear women who have the uncanny ability to think like a man, yet be all woman. These women have the special ability to appreciate a man as he is, without trying to change that man to be more like them. They can relish in a man's world without feeling slighted or ignored.

Here are some of the traits that I have seen in this kind of woman:

> 1. **This special woman knows that one of the greatest needs of a man is respect**, and she is wise enough to know that if she gives him that respect, she gets what she wants like love, affection, liberty, and anything else.

157

2. **This special woman knows how to come near her husband** and snuggle with him while he is watching the Super Bowl game, be quiet, enjoy it, and have all of the food and drinks available. She knows how to get her pleasure by just being with him. She is also feminine enough to know not to sit in the room when there are a bunch of guys visiting to watch the game as well, and she doesn't get an attitude about it. She enjoys being a woman, and she wants her man to be a man.

3. **This special woman knows that men think straightforwardly**, and she sees this as a gift from God to solve problems quicker, and she doesn't get offended by it. She, therefore, provides information to her husband about problems, bills, etc., in a straightforward, orderly fashion.

4. **This special woman knows that men like for you to express your feelings, desires, and needs in a concrete, straightforward, and truthful manner** instead of him being forced to try to guess and figure out what you want or need.

5. **This special woman knows that men desire sex more than women do**, so instead of being sickened by this thought, she prepares herself to be ready to satisfy his needs. If she is not really in the mood, or even if she doesn't get much physical satisfaction from the episode, her satisfaction comes from satisfying him.

I can go on and on. Men love women who can think like them, while at the same time be all woman because to some degree, it is a man's world — but without you, it wouldn't be any fun.

Blessings,

Papa

P.T.:

♦ *"Let the wife make the husband glad to come home, and let him make her sorry to see him leave."*
—Martin Luther

♦ *"If there is such a thing as a good marriage, it is because it resembles friendship rather than love."*
—Michel Eyquem de Montaigne

BIBLE GEM: "Let the husband render unto the wife due benevolence: and likewise also the wife unto the husband."
—I Corinthians 7:3

TALK TO GOD: Holy Father, Give me the ability to think like a man but be all woman. In Jesus Christ's precious name. Amen.

BOOK: The Power of Being a Woman: Mastering the Art of Femininity, by Michelle McKinney Hammond

CHECK IT OUT: www.biblicalwomanhoodonline.com

HOW TO WIN AT RELATIONSHIPS (AND NEVER GET HURT)

Letter Thirty

Dear Daughters & YBW:

I trust that God is speaking to your heart through these letters.

Today, I am writing to you about how to win at relationships and never get hurt. It never ceases to amaze me how many young ladies walk around with broken hearts and broken lives. I really believe that this does not have to be the case. I believe young ladies don't have to walk around with their heads down, full of shame and guilt, depressed, bitter and full of negative attitudes toward every black man they see. I believe young women can be happy, cheerful, and victorious if they would simply apply the following in regard to relationships:

> 1. **Don't have many relationships in the first place.** You don't need to have fifteen boyfriends before you get married. Rachel in the Bible only had one, and she married him.

> 2. **Never give a man your eyes**; never give a man your heart; never give a man your body before you are married. I like the title of Big Boom's new book, which is: *If You Want Closure in Your Relationship, Start with Your Legs.* You see, young ladies, it is very simple: if you don't give a man anything, he has

nothing over you, and you won't get hurt. Now, he may be hurt that you didn't let him have his way, but you can walk away with a smile on your face, a pep in your step, and a song on your lips.

3. **Pray and meditate on the Bible.** As I have said elsewhere in this book, "If you do the right thing, you will always be in the right place at the right time." I like the umbrella illustration that Bill Gothard uses regarding the protection of God. If you obey the Word of God, you are under God's umbrella of protection. If you don't obey the Word of God, it's going to rain on you.

4. **Keep a strong relationship with your parents and siblings if you can.** These relationships alone will keep you so busy that you will not have time to get into a relationship that is going to hurt you. The same thing goes for your church family. Find a good, Bible-believing, Christ-honoring church, and be faithful to its services and special meetings. It will be a great source of strength and protection for you in these last days.

5. **Let the Lord be your constant "partner."** Jesus Christ promises you that He *"will never leave thee, nor forsake thee"* (Hebrews 13:5b). Keep a strong fellowship with the Lord, and you will be so filled with Him that you will never have a hunger so deep that you would get into a bad relationship that could cause you hurt and pain.

Yours for Never Getting Hurt,

Papa

P.T.:

♦ "It is often hard to bear the tears that we ourselves have caused."
— Marcel Proust

♦ "On the sands of life sorrow treads heavily, and leaves a print time cannot wash away."
— Henry Neele

♦ "Never let the hand you hold, hold you down."
— Author Unknown

BIBLE GEM: "Marriage is honorable in all, and the bed undefiled: but whoremongers and adulterers God will judge."
— Hebrews 13:4

TALK TO GOD: Holy Father, Give me wisdom and understanding in the relationships that I choose. Help me to always keep a great, fruitful, loving relationship with You, and to never forget that You are my constant partner. Protect me from getting hurt and from falling into meaningless relationships. In Jesus Christ's magnificent name. Amen.

BOOK: *Falling in Love with Jesus: Abandoning Yourself to the Greatest Romance of Your Life*, by Dee Brestin & Kathy Troccoli

CHECK IT OUT: www.juanitabynum.com

HOW NOT TO BECOME A VICTIM

Letter Thirty-One

Dear Daughters & YBW:

May the Lord's blessings and protection be upon you today.

As you know, I pray daily for your protection. Unfortunately, we live in very perilous times with a pervert living on what seems like every corner. My heart is broken daily when I hear the news about young girls being abused by a relative, raped by a pervert, or abducted by a sociopath. Sometimes when I hear of these atrocities, not only do I get angry at the perverts, but I get angry at the parents for being negligent. Sometimes, I also get angry at the poor victim for being in the wrong place at the wrong time. You can't prevent an idiot from choosing your house for a home invasion, but there are some things that you can do to not become a victim of a violent crime:

1. **Stay with your parents until you are married**. Years ago, my two sisters ran into some problems when they left home as single women. I, being the concerned older brother, encouraged my parents to get the girls back home with them until they got married. They did that, and things worked out better for them. Both of my sisters later married police officers, with one of the officers being a Gospel minister, as well.

2. **Try to do everything you need to do outside the home before the sun goes down.** When the sun goes down, the perverts come out. I realize many people don't want to accept this fact, but the truth of the matter is, there are many people in our communities, who are simply demon possessed. There is no other way to explain the atrocities that are happening in our communities today.

3. **When you have to go somewhere, go with your parents, your siblings, or some close friends, and carry a cell phone with you.** There was a time in our country when a young lady could take a walk alone out on the country road to get some exercise and fresh air; but friend, that time is long gone. Don't be foolish, wherever you go, have someone with you.

4. **Don't smile at or greet men you don't know.** I hate to be cold, but many men are so perverted in their minds that just because you smiled at them and/or greeted them, they think you like them or something. If you don't know them, keep stepping, and as the Bible says in Proverbs 4:25, *"Let thine eyes look right on, and let thine eyelids look straight before thee."*

5. Speaking of eyes, some young women have a serious problem with wandering eyes. **Don't let men make eye contact with you.** The reason is, as I said before: The perverted minds of men think that the eye contact that you are letting them have with you, means that you are somehow interested in them. I know that this sounds strange to you, but believe it.

6. **Let your parents know when you get on and off the internet.** If something evil pops up on the computer, report it to your parents. Be accountable to your parents, and tell them what happens. Don't chat with anyone on the internet because oftentimes, you do not know who you are chatting with. Too many young girls' minds have been blown away by crooks and perverts via the internet. Don't let this happen to you.

7. **Stay home.** Don't think that being in the street all the time is cool. Stay home sometimes, and find interesting and constructive things to do there. Also, while you are at home, make sure the doors and windows are locked, and the alarm is on.

I hate to sound like an alarmist, but we are living in perilous times. I do not want to see you and your family go through the terror, heartache, and pain that so many other families have been through. These are just some tips to help you stay safe. Please see my P.T. for more info on how to keep yourself from becoming a victim.

Yours for Safety,

Papa

P.T.:

♦ *Don't take rides from strangers — male or female.*

♦ *Don't wait around in dark places.*

- Don't give your phone number or other personal information to strangers.

- Let your parents know your work and/or school schedule.

- Say "NO" and mean it.

- Don't accept gifts from strangers.

- Be very careful about engaging in conversation with the opposite sex.

- Feel comfortable telling your parents or other guardians anything.

- If you must work overtime, let your parents know.

BIBLE GEM: "The horse is prepared against the day of battle: but safety is of the Lord."
—Proverbs 21:31

TALK TO GOD: Holy Father, I pray that You would please protect me and keep me safe in this wicked world. Give me Your strength, Your wisdom, and Your guidance to go through each day, and help me to make the right decisions in everything that I do. In Jesus Christ's name, I pray. Amen.

BOOK: Not An Easy Target: Paxton Quigley's Self-Protection for Women, by Paxton Quigley

CHECK IT OUT: www.paxtonquigley.com

10 THINGS SOME WOMEN DO THAT ABSOLUTELY TURN MEN OFF

Letter Thirty-Two

Dear Daughters & YBW:

I trust that you are doing well.

My dear mother and I have had our differences down through the years, but one thing that I really appreciate about my mother is that she carried herself with class throughout my upbringing. What I mean by that is that there were just some things that my mother didn't do and that she didn't allow my sisters to do while we were growing up. You see, my mother was a part of the last generation of black women who were raised to be chaste and to carry themselves with class and dignity. This is not to say that there aren't women who carry themselves like that today, but they are certainly few and far between.

Now, I am getting ready to make a few people mad. Some of the things that I am going to mention below may sound comical, but they irritate most men:

> 1. **Announcing what you are going to do while you are in the bathroom** or somehow indicating what you did in the bathroom. Just saying, "excuse me while I go to the ladies' room," will suffice. I was dating a

young woman once, who in the course of our conversation, said, "Excuse me, I have to go boo-boo." She thought she was being natural — I thought she had lost her mind. When I questioned her about her announcing her business, she blurted out, "What! That's only natural." Well, it killed what little feelings of romance I had for her that day.

2. **Body odors.** Nothing will turn a man off quicker than body odors coming from the woman that he is with. Take a shower daily — sometimes twice a day, and put some type of body deodorant on to help you keep your odors under control.

3. Another turn off is **bad breath.** Get your teeth checked. Floss and brush your teeth thoroughly every day. Use Listerine. Keep mints on you. I remember when I was a little boy, my grandmother Beaman, and my mother always had some Juicy Fruit gum or some Doublemint gum to keep their breath fresh, and to help keep a little rambunctious boy quiet in church. Don't let your breath blow your man away.

4. **Flatulence**. Now, I am going to be as nice as I can about this. Please do not commit the crime of flatulence. Now if you don't know what that means, you need to look it up in the dictionary. I know, I know, you say men do it. Well, it is just one of those things that men can get away with, but women cannot. It is a big turn off. If you start having problems, go to the restroom, and stay there until the storm passes over. I never heard my mother commit the crime of flatulence. Never.

5. **Cursing.** It has never been respectable for women to curse in our society, even though more and more women are doing it. No matter how pretty you are, a filthy mouth makes you ugly.

6. **Smoking and Drinking.** "Good women don't smoke, don't chew, and they don't run with those who do," and they don't drink either. They don't do it because it makes them look like loose women.

7. **Your Visitor.** Men are not turned off by a woman's period; they are just turned off if it changes the woman into a witch once a month. It does not have to be a dramatic ordeal every month. You must make a decision and choose, by the grace of God, to take control of this area of your life. If Oprah Winfrey and Vanna White can put on a smile and be cheerful and perform in a professional manner for the hour or so that they are doing their shows even during this period of their lives, you can as well. If it can be done for one hour, it can be done for five hours. If it can be done for five hours, it can be done for twenty-four hours. If you have to, force yourself to communicate to your husband ahead of time that your period is about to begin, and that there might be a dip in how you might feel. This way he can prepare himself and compensate accordingly. I know, I know, you want him to always know what is going on with you. Well, unfortunately, most men don't operate like that; you will most likely need to tell him. Also, your husband will want you to handle these issues with your daughters. Accidents, in this area, are inexcusable.

8. **Fake hair and fake stuff.** Another big turn off for men is fake hair, fake nails, fake posteriors, and fake breasts, etc. I won't deal with the rest of it right now, but let me just deal with the fake hair. Most men would rather see you with a short natural afro than with a bunch of horse hair, weaved into your head — honestly. The man feels, at least, what he sees is what he gets. Most men like real everything, unless they have fake stuff themselves.

9. **Lack of femininity.** Sadly, today, we have men acting more feminine than women. If these aren't the last days, I don't know what is. Anyway, real men desire to be with women to enjoy their unique femininity. A man does not want you to be just as rough and wild as he is. Embrace your natural femininity, and you will have a man eating out of your hands.

10. Believe it or not, most men are turned off by **women who are desperate,** and who express their desperateness by trying to entice men by showing as much skin as possible. When it comes to marrying time, he is going to probably go for the woman who knows how to dress modestly, and still look fantastic.

Today, many men do not have the guts to tell a woman anything that he thinks she won't like, and quite frankly, many men are afraid of women — for whatever reason. But believe me, these are the top 10 things that turn men off. Don't do them, and you will never have a problem keeping a good man happy.

Walk with class,

Papa

P.T.:

♦ "People may doubt what you say, but they will always believe what you do."
—Selected

♦ "If you do not tell the truth about yourself, you cannot tell it about other people."
—Virginia Woolf

♦ "Success can make you go one of two ways. It can make you a prima donna, or it can smooth the edges, take away the insecurities, let the nice things come out."
—Barbara Walters

♦ "Being a lady is an attitude."
—Chuck Woolery

♦ "I think a woman gets more if she acts feminine."
—Nancy Reagan

BIBLE GEM: "A gracious woman retaineth honour."
—Proverbs 11:16a

TALK TO GOD: Holy Father, I pray in the name of the Lord Jesus Christ that You would help me to be a woman of class and dignity. Help me to carry myself well in front of all people. In Jesus Christ's name. Amen.

BOOK: His Lady, by TD Jakes

CHECK IT OUT: www.spiritledwoman.com

MEN FOLK!

Letter Thirty-Three

Dear Daughters & YBW:

In my book, ***Letters To Young Black Men,*** I wrote a rather controversial letter entitled, **Women Folk!** Well, in this letter, I am going to share with you some inside knowledge regarding the men folk. This will cause some men to get angry with me, because I am going to break the code of silence about the psychological tricks and games that men play on women. That is alright, however, because my sharing these crucial points will save you years of heartache and pain.

1. **You need to understand this — the thoughts that most men have about you are not good**. They will try to make you think they have pure, innocent thoughts toward you, but that is not the case. What most men want from you is casual sex, and if they can get that from you, without marrying you, they will do that. Sad to say, some "Christian" men are just as bad as worldly men. If a man can have sex with you, enjoy all the pleasures you can give him, and get away with it, he will do it. A man's mentality is, "why buy the cow, when the milk is free." There are very few men who have noble and pure thoughts about you.

2. **The way to a man's heart is not through his stomach; rather, it is through showing him respect**. To a man, respect is more important than even your

love. Unfortunately, so many women waste their time trying to win a man over with their body, with their food, and with their money; yet the main thing that a man wants from you is your unadulterated respect. The simple verses in the Bible such as Ephesians 5:22, 23, 24, 33, Colossians 3:18, and I Peter 3:1, all consist of God trying to tell women that the secret to a man's heart is showing the man respect. This is the same thing that God expects from mankind — respect, reverence, and honor. If you give a man respect, that man will give you the world.

3. **Many men do not believe you mean "No" when you say "No."** You are the gatekeeper. If you don't open the gate, the dawgs won't come in. My friend, Pastor Cuthbertson, mentioned to me the other day, when I was discussing this book with him, that young women need to learn how to say "no" more forcibly. Because if you don't say it like you mean it, that man is going to continue to work on you.

4. **Remember, young ladies, you are the ultimate prize**. Don't settle for a man that is not up to your standards. Keep your standards high.

5. If you get married, **you need to marry a faithful man**; and a faithful man is hard to find. Pray hard.

6. **Think with your head, and not with your emotions**. Men are attracted to women physically, primarily. A woman has an innate, God-given desire to have a man in her life. Don't let your innate God-

given desire make you do foolish things to try to get a man outside of the will of God.

7. **Everything that glitters ain't gold**. A man may be fine and handsome on the outside, he may be well-spoken, he may be driving a great-looking car, he may even look like he has some money, and he may be as charming as he can be, but he may also be nothing but a no-good scoundrel, who is just going to do you harm. What you want to get is a man who is going to be faithful, trustworthy, loving, have the ability to lead a family, and have the ability to provide well for you and the children. If you fool around and get yourself a man who is fine on the outside, but full of selfishness, pride, bitterness, and who is abusive then you will have hell to pay. Mark my words.

Well, daughters, I can write a book on this subject, but for now, just take heed to this advice and don't let the dawgs bite.

Handle the Men Folk well,

P.T.:

♦ *"There are easier things in life than trying to find a nice guy...like nailing jelly to a tree for example."*
　　　　　　　　　　　　　　　　　　—Selected

♦ *"Don't ask God to do what you want. Ask God to do what is right."*　　　　　　　　　—Selected

177

♦ *"No man is worth your tears, but once you find one that is, he won't make you cry."*

—Selected

BIBLE GEM: *"Most men will proclaim every one his own goodness: but a faithful man who can find?"*

—Proverbs 20:6

TALK TO GOD: *Heavenly Father, I pray that You would give me the wisdom to help me deal with the men folk well. In Jesus Christ's name. Amen*

BOOK: *For Women Only: What You Need to Know About the Inner Lives of Men,* by Shaunti Feldhahn

CHECK IT OUT: www.shaunti.com

STRAIGHT TALK ABOUT SEX

Letter Thirty-Four

Dear Daughters & YBW:

Sadly, thousands of young black women down through the years have lost their precious virginity before marriage, have had babies out of wedlock, and have experienced untold shame and pain, simply because their parents and other family members have not had the guts to sit down with them, look them squarely in their faces and tell them the truth about sex (not "the birds and the bees," whatever that may be). The truth is, parents are having sex all of the time — even some who are not married are having sex. Sex produced the children that they have, yet they have a problem telling their children how they got here, thus making a mystery out of it.

My dear parents, bless their hearts, did the best they could with the knowledge they had. But my dad never talked with me about sex, or about the "birds and the bees" for that matter; and the only thing I heard from my mother was, "If you are going to have sex, use some protection." Well, to a young, lost, red-blooded hoodlum, as I was — little did she know — that was like saying "sic 'em" to a dog. Since they did not sit down with me and tell me the truth about sex, it became one of those "forbidden things" that I wanted to experience. Unfortunately, what I learned about sex, I learned on the street, and that resulted in a lot of people getting hurt.

So, girls, here is the lowdown, or the high up, on sex, (and parents, if you find what I am saying too graphic, before you write me to fuss at me, you need to turn off BET):

1. **God made sex**. God made sex very pleasurable and interesting so that people would do it a lot, inside the bonds of marriage, to obey His command to *"multiply and replenish the earth"* (Genesis 1:28). There is no mystery about sex.

2. **Sex is very straightforward.** God has given a man a penis and God has given a woman a vagina, designed to receive the penis. There is no secret to this and there is nothing dirty about this. When it is time for you to have sex, once you are married, you will know what to do. It will be just as natural as when a baby comes out of the womb knowing how to suck his or her mother's breasts. Once the man ejaculates his sperm inside the vagina, the possibility exists for the woman to get pregnant.

   You see, there is no mystery about it. Sex is not some dirty little secret. This is important to know, lest you get curious as Eve did in the garden, and then you disobey God and mess up your life.

3. **Sex, of any kind, outside of marriage, although momentarily pleasurable, brings pain, hurt, and disillusionment to you, the young lady, because you will carry the brunt of the burden, as well as the children born out of wed-lock.**

I hate to close this letter with this, but even though in God's sight, the young man and young woman who have sex outside of marriage are equally guilty, in our society, the young woman is the one who has the most to lose. Remember the story about the chicken and the pig. The man is just making a donation; you are making a total sacrifice.

Yours for Being Smart About Sex,

P.T.:

♦ *"The Bible has a word to describe 'safe sex.' It's called marriage."*
　　　　　　　　　　　　　　　—*Gary Smalley & John Trent*

♦ *"God's wounds cure, sin's kisses kill."*
　　　　　　　　　　　　　　　—*William Gurnall*

♦ *"Purity doesn't happen by accident; it requires obedience to God... Without purity, God's gift of sexuality becomes a destruction game."*
　　　　　　　　　　　　　　　—*Joshua Harris*

♦ *"While purity before marriage consists in holding ourselves from one another in obedience to God, purity after marriage consists in giving ourselves to and for each other in obedience to God."*
　　　　　　　　　　　　　　　—*Elisabeth Elliot*

♦ *"If you truly desire to live a lifestyle of purity, you'll learn the secret of speaking boldly."*
　　　　　　　　　　　　　　　—*Dannah Gresh*

BIBLE GEM: "Now concerning the things whereof ye wrote unto me: It is good for a man not to touch a woman. Nevertheless, to avoid fornication, let every

181

man have his own wife and let every woman have her own husband."

TALK TO GOD: Dear God, thank you for helping me to understand the truth about sex. Help me not to have sex outside the bonds of marriage. Help me to keep myself pure and holy for Your glory, praise, and honor. In Jesus Christ's name. Amen.

BOOK: *And the Bride Wore White: Seven Secrets to Sexual Purity*, by Dannah Gresh

CHECK IT OUT: www.purefreedom.org

ON THE POWER OF A CONSISTENTLY CHEERFUL SPIRIT AND PERSONALITY

Letter Thirty-Five

Dear Daughters & YBW:

Jesus Christ gave all of His children a command in St. John 16:33:

"These things I have spoken unto you, that in me ye might have peace. In the world ye shall have tribulation: but be of good cheer; I have overcome the world."

Also, while in jail, mind you, the Apostle Paul said in Philippians 4:4: *"Rejoice in the Lord alway: and again I say, Rejoice."*

So, we see here that regardless of the situation one is in, God expects, yea, commands us, to be cheerful and joyful at all times. This includes both men and women, boys and girls. I believe it is a slap in God's face for Christians to walk around with sad faces — defeated and depressed.

Daughters, I recall that when your mother and I were first married, I began to see a disturbing pattern in Meriqua's behavior. She was cheerful and happy for two weeks out of the month, and then as her period approached, her attitude and personality changed dramatically to a more negative personality. This caused no small problem in our marriage.

So after about two years of this, I had a revelation, and the revelation was this — God never intended for a wife to be an angel for six months out of the year, and a devil for the other six months. I then shared with her that she, through prayer, would have to get that area of her life under control and begin to simply obey the Word of God by being cheerful and joyful no matter what. It took a while, but she got better.

Daughters, do not believe the devil's lies that you have a right to have a bad attitude and spirit just because you are going through something, or because you are not feeling well. That kind of mentality will keep you defeated throughout your life. The people around you will be miserable, and it can destroy your vital relationships. You must make up your mind that no matter what is going on in your life, you are going to be cheerful and joyful at all times, and that you are going to be steady and consistent every day. So, practice having a joyful spirit always. God will use that to impact people's lives for the Kingdom, it makes for a very happy home, and it will open many doors for you throughout your life.

Stay Sweet,

P.T.:

♦ "Happiness is neither within us only, or without us; it is the union of ourselves with God."
—Pascal

♦ "Self pity is the most miserable party to go to, because, in case you haven't noticed, you're the only one who is there..."

—Joyce Meyer

♦ Happiness is an inside job."

—Selected

♦ "I'm fulfilled in what I do... I never thought that a lot of money or fine clothes — the finer things of life — would make you happy. My concept of happiness is to be filled in a spiritual sense."

—Coretta Scott-King

♦ "Now and then it's good to pause in our pursuit of happiness and just be happy."

—Anonymous

♦ "Most people are about as happy as they make up their minds to be."

—Abraham Lincoln

♦ "Sometimes we are limited more by attitude than by opportunities."   —Anonymous

♦ "Joy is the echo of God's life within us."

—Joseph Marmion

BIBLE GEM: "For the joy of the Lord is your strength."
—Nehemiah 8:10b

TALK TO GOD: Dear God, please help me to always be joyful, cheerful, and sweet, no matter what the circumstances are. Thank You Lord for everything You've done for me. In Jesus Christ's name. Amen.

BOOK: The Power of Being Positive, by Joyce Meyer

CHECK IT OUT: www.joyfulchristianministries.com

GOOD GIRLS ALWAYS FINISH FIRST

Letter Thirty-Six

Dear Daughters & YBW:

If you listen to the world through the media, etc., you would think that the bad girls always finish first, and the good girls are left behind and forgotten. This reminds me of a passage of scripture that was a great comfort to me when I was younger. (Please read the entire chapter at your convenience. I will only quote a portion of it here) It is Psalm 73:1-7 & 16-17:

> *"Truly God is good to Israel, even to such as are of a clean heart. But as for me, my feet were almost gone; my steps had well nigh slipped. For I was envious at the foolish, when I saw the prosperity of the wicked. For there are no bands in their death: but their strength is firm. They are not in trouble as other men; neither are they plagued like other men. Therefore pride compasseth them about as a chain; violence covereth them as a garment. Their eyes stand out with fatness: they have more than heart could wish...When I thought to know this, it was too painful for me; Until I went into the sanctuary of God; then understood I their end."*

GOOD GIRLS ALWAYS FINISH FIRST. Don't misunderstand me. Some bad girls learn from their mistakes and turn to the Lord and become good girls and win in the end too. But good girls always, always finish first. Here are some things that good girls do to finish first:

1. **Good girls obey and listen to their parents.** They have the wisdom to understand that their parents know what is best for them. The Bible says in Ephesians 6:1-3: *"Children, obey your parents in the Lord: for this is right. Honour thy father and mother; which is the first commandment with promise; That it may be well with thee, and thou mayest live long on the earth."*

2. **Good girls love the Lord Jesus Christ**, they obey His Word, and they serve Him through their local church. The verse that motivates them is John 14:15, *"If you love me keep my commandments."*

3. **Good girls focus their attention on doing well in school** and helping with important causes. They keep themselves busy helping other people, and taking advantage of learning experiences.

4. **Good girls do not allow young men to disrespect them** by letting them kiss on them, hug on them, touch them, or partake of any other kind of illicit sexual activity, in any way, shape, form, or fashion before marriage. They do not allow this activity, because they know that if they allow the young man an inch, he will take a mile.

5. **Good girls dress appropriately for every situation.** They dress modestly. They have the class

and the inside knowledge that they do not have to reveal their body to appear attractive. In fact, they know, the less they show, the more attractive they are and the more respected they are. I Timothy 2:9a says: ***"In like manner also, that women adorn themselves in modest apparel..."***

Good girls are "bad" in the good sense. Good girls always finish first — Always.

Stay a Good Girl, Though the Stars Fall,

Papa

P.T.:

♦ *"There are few good women who do not tire of their role."* —*Francois de La Rochefoucauld*

♦ *"Whatever any one does or says, I must be good."* —*Marcus Aurelius Antoninus*

BIBLE GEM: "Well done, thou good and faithful servant...enter thou into the joy of thy Lord." —*Matthew 25:21*

TALK TO GOD: Dear God, help me to be a good girl and help me not to be envious of the wicked who seem to prosper because I know that through You I will win every time, not for show but for Your glory. In Jesus Christ's name. Amen.

BOOK: God's Trophy Woman: You Are Blessed & Highly Favored, by Jacqueline Jakes

CHECK IT OUT: www.womenbygrace.com

AND FOR THE YOUNG WOMEN WHO ARE ALREADY MARRIED

by Meriqua Whyte

Letter Thirty-Seven

Dear Daughters & YBW:

In this letter, I am going to allow my wife of 20 years, Meriqua, to share some things with those young ladies who are already married. Take it away, Meriqua:

Dear Daughters and Young Ladies:

There are some things I wish someone had told me before I got married as to what my role should be as a wife and mother. Because I did not receive this training before I got married, I unfortunately made many mistakes. Thankfully, the Lord has used my husband to teach me how to be a wife and mother. Here are some things that I have learned:

> 1. **Have a cheerful spirit and attitude at all times.** Your feelings change each day but you have to learn to act based upon the Word of God, and not on how you feel.

> 2. **Respect and honor your husband.** The wife is told in Ephesians 5:33 to *"see that she reverence her husband."* A man wants respect from his wife above anything else. Young ladies, pray and ask the Lord to help you to be respectful toward your husband.

3. **Have a meek and quiet spirit.** The Bible says in I Peter 3:1-4: *"Likewise, ye wives, be in subjection to your own husbands; that, if any obey not the word, they also may without the word be won by the conversation of the wives; While they behold your chaste conversation coupled with fear. Whose adorning let it not be that outward adorning of plaiting the hair, and of wearing of gold, or of putting on of apparel; But let it be the hidden man of the heart, in that which is not corruptible, even the ornament of a meek and quiet spirit, which is in the sight of God of great price."* Having a meek and quiet spirit is not answering back, rolling the eyes, or blowing. A meek and quiet spirit goes a long way. It will keep your household peaceful.

4. **Do not lie to your husband under any circumstances.** Lying destroys the foundation of any relationship. Colossians 3:9 says: *"Lie not one to another, seeing that ye have put off the old man with his deeds."* Lying will probably do more damage to your relationship than anything else. Whatever you do, don't lie to your husband or to anyone else about anything. "Honesty is the best policy."

5. **Submit yourself to your husband.** Another word for "submit" is obedience. The Bible tells us in Ephesians 5:22 & 23: *"Wives, submit yourselves unto your own husbands, as unto the Lord. For the husband is the head of the wife, even as Christ is the head of the church: and he is the saviour of the body."* If you obey your husband, then you are obeying God; therein lies your blessing.

6. **Love, nurture, and care for your children.** Psalm 127:3 says: ***"Lo, children are an heritage of the Lord: and the fruit of the womb is his reward."*** Thank the Lord daily for your children, and pray for wisdom in training them in the right and Godly way.

7. **Keep your house clean.** Figure out the best way to balance housework, taking care of the children, and working an outside job. But keep the house clean.

8. **Meditate upon the Word of God.** Here are some portions of Scripture on which to meditate upon throughout the day, which will help you to be the wife and mother that God would have you to be:

- I Peter 3:1-6
- Ephesians 5:22-33
- Colossians 3:18
- Titus 2:1-5
- Proverbs 31:10-31
- Proverbs 14:1
- Proverbs 12:4

I am ashamed to say that I have failed God and my husband in all of these areas, at times in our marriage. But when I have applied these simple principles in our family, our home is a little Heaven on earth. Daughters and young ladies, contrary to what the world may be teaching you, we must do our part in our marriages and families because whether we want to accept this responsibility or not, as the old saying goes, "the wife and the mother is the spirit of the home, and she sets the tone for the home."

Also, before I close, let me share a thought with you, and that is, I believe many women are unhappy in their marriages because they are not keeping the vows they made to God on their wedding day, and believe it or not, God is holding them accountable. (See Bible Gem in the P.T. section of this letter.)

Let me encourage you, that after reading this letter, to obtain a copy of the vows you made to God on your wedding day, if you have forgotten them, and read them over at least once a week to refresh your memory as to what you need to do as a wife because God has "no pleasure in fools," that is, one who does not keep a promise or vow made to Him.

Let's do the mature thing: be committed to our marriage vows, respect our husbands, love and care for our children, and God will reward us in time to come. Proverbs 31:25 says *"**Strength and honour are her clothing; and she shall rejoice in time to come.**"*

Daughters and YBW, God loves you and I love you. The Lord wants you to have a happy home and marriage — one that will honor His name. If you apply the things above, you will have a happy marriage and home, and a blessed life.

For a Happy Home,

Meriqua

P.T.:

♦ *"The family is a haven in a heartless world."*
        —Attributed to Christopher Lasch

- "There is no lovely, friendly and charming relationship, communion or company than a good marriage."

  —Martin Luther

- "To keep your marriage brimming,
    With love in the loving cup,
    Whenever you're wrong admit it;
    Whenever you're right shut up."

  —Ogden Nash

BIBLE GEM: "When thou vowest a vow unto God, defer not to pay it; for he hath no pleasure in fools: pay that which thou hast vowed. Better is it that thou shouldest not vow, than that thou shouldest vow and not pay. Suffer not thy mouth to cause thy flesh to sin; neither say thou before the angel, that it was an error: wherefore should God be angry at thy voice, and destroy the work of thy hands?"

—Ecclesiastes 5: 4-6

TALK TO GOD: Dear God, thank You for blessing me with the man that I have and the children that I have. Please help me to love and respect my husband, and please help me to love and take care of my children. In Jesus Christ's name. Amen.

BOOKS: The Proper Care and Feeding of Husbands, by Dr. Laura Schlessinger

Me, Obey Him?, by Elizabeth Rice Hanford

CHECK IT OUT: www.familylife.com

PAPA'S PET PEEVES

(*7 Miscellanous Rules for Young Black Women*)

Letter Thirty-Eight

Dear Daughters & YBW:

I pray that you are doing well today, and I hope that you are enjoying your life.

I have some pet peeves in regard to the young ladies in my household, and I thought I would share them with you as well. These things are not popular in our society. But as you already know, I do not care about being popular. These things come from a loving father's heart. I love you and I want the very best for you. Here they are:

1. **Don't put relaxers in your hair until you are at least sixteen years old,** unless you have very thick hair, and then fourteen might be alright. "Be happy nappy" — that is, be natural until your hair is strong enough to handle the harsh chemicals in relaxers. I believe that many girls' hair is ruined for life by the time they are fourteen or fifteen years old because of parents allowing harsh chemicals to be put in their children's hair at such an early age. Stay natural until your hair is strong enough to handle the chemicals.

2. **Don't get your ears pierced until at least sixteen years of age.** You ask why? Because I said so.

3. **Stay Busy! Stay busy! Stay busy!** Keep your mind occupied doing constructive things. After you finish your school work, do your chores; after you do your chores, learn how to play an instrument; after that, learn a new language. Yes, rest, relax, exercise, have some down time; but keep moving. It is harder for the devil and unscrupulous young men to get you if you stay busy.

4. **Let your siblings be your best friends.** They won't lead you astray because they are going in the same way.

5. **Have two lists to live by:** a **permanent list** of things to do each day that you do in an orderly fashion, and a **running list** of new things to do each day. For example, on your **permanent list,** you can have simple things such as:

   1. Wake up at 6:00 AM
   2. Pray
   3. Read the Bible
   4. Exercise
   5. Shower
   6. Clean up your room
   7. Do chores
   8. Go to school

This list of eight serves like a rocket-launcher to get your day going.

Your **running list** for a Monday could look like this:

1. Help pick up groceries
2. Clean the garage
3. Go to piano lessons

6. **Be organized in all that you do.** Where there is confusion and disorder, the devil is at work. Remember, ***"God is not the author of confusion."***

7. **Pray! Think! Do!** When you have a problem, project or task to do, here is how you can successfully reach your goal.

   1. Pray about it. Ask God to help you with it, and He will.
   2. Think through it. Plan your work.
   3. Then do it. Work your plan.

Sweethearts, don't allow your minds to become confused. Keep yourself organized, and do things in an orderly fashion. Stay clean, neat, and organized.

These are just some of my pet peeves. Eat the meat and leave the bones.

Love and a Long Life,

Papa

P.T.:

♦ *"A woman is like a tea bag — you can't tell how strong she is until you put her in hot water."*
                                        —*Nancy Reagan*

♦ *"A smile is a wrinkle that shouldn't be removed."*
—Selected

♦ *"The really tough thing about true humility is that you can't brag about it."*
—Gene Brown

BIBLE GEM: *"What? Know ye not that your body is the temple of the Holy Ghost which is in you, which ye have of God, and ye are not your own? For ye are bought with a price: therefore glorify God in your body, and in your spirit, which are God's."*
—1 Corinthians 6:19-20

TALK TO GOD: *Holy Father God, help me to live my life on purpose, to be organized, and to stay busy for Your glory. In Jesus Christ's name, I pray. Amen.*

BOOK: *Look Great Feel Great,* by Joyce Meyer

CHECK IT OUT: *www.donnarichardson.com*

IF YOU ARE HURTING...

Letter Thirty-Nine

Dear YBW:

My prayer is that you are doing well and that you have never experienced some of the terrible things that we so unfortunately, and so often, hear about in the news today, such as rape, teenage pregnancy with the father leaving you behind to carry the load, sexual abuse by people you trusted, etc. Quite frankly, I do not know how people cope with such things, without the grace of God. But if you have experienced such a traumatic thing in your life, there is hope and there is help.

One of the amazing things that I have learned in life is that God has given each of us special gifts and callings to be a blessing to others, such as: the gift of mercy, the gift of administration, the gift of giving, the gift of evangelism, and the gift of prophecy. Well, my gift is the gift of prophecy. Many people think today that the gift of prophecy is just about predicting people's future, etc. But the gift of prophecy is more about preventing problems in the first place; this book is more about prevention, than it is about recovery. My goal in this book is to get you to the point where you never put yourself in a position to be hurt in the first place: a position of power and liberty.

But if you are hurting right now, we have some help for you. "There is a balm in Gilead." We have included in this book a list of ministries that can help you cope with, and recover from whatever you may be going through. The Motherboard, on page 211, will help you get back on your feet and be the conqueror that God wants you to be.

Hold on, help is on the way,

Papa

P.T.:

In the meantime, please visit www.hopefortheheart.org.

♦ *"Your misery is your ministry."*
—Juanita Bynum

♦ *"When down in the mouth remember Jonah — he came out all right!"*
—Thomas Edison

♦ *"We must accept finite disappointment, but we must never lose infinite hope."*
—Martin Luther King, Jr.

♦ *"Character cannot be developed in ease and quiet. Only through experience of trial and suffering can the soul be strengthened, vision cleared, ambition inspired, and success achieved."*
—Helen Keller

BIBLE GEM: "Casting all your care upon him; for he careth for you."
—1 Peter 5:7

TALK TO GOD: Dear God, even though I have been hurt, I thank You that "weeping may endure for a night, but joy cometh in the morning." Please heal all of my pain, and help me not to remain a victim but to become a victor through You. Help me not to be bitter or angry towards those who have hurt me, but help me to forgive them. I thank You that You will always be with me. In Jesus Christ's powerful name. Amen.

BOOK: *Get Over It and On with It: How to Get Up When Life Knocks You Down*, by Michelle McKinney Hammond

CHECK IT OUT: *www.hopefortheheart.org*

A TRIBUTE TO MY FATHER

by Daniella Whyte

Letter Forty

Dear YBW:

Greetings!

I trust that this series of Letters have been a help and a blessing to you. I hope that you will read it, read it again, and then pass it on to another young black woman who may be struggling to find her way in this sometimes confusing and hostile world.

Below, my daughter, Daniella, who has been such a tremendous help in my ministry, and especially in helping me to write this book, wanted to share a word with you before we go. Take it away, Danni:

My dad is special. God has put fathers on this earth to lead us, guide us, love us, and encourage us — and also to pull us back when we begin to go astray. A lot of people underestimate the power of a father, but fathers always have a great impact on the lives of their children.

My dad is a great father. He has taught me a lot of things, all of which are in this book. I am thankful that my father has a lot of wisdom and knowledge that he has passed down to me, so that I can pass down to my children. As he always says, each generation is supposed to be better than

the last one, and one person can make an entire generation better.

There has never been a man like my father. He loves me, takes care of me, and teaches me the right things of life. I take after him in a lot of ways, like in my leadership, writing, and communication. We both have a similar sense of humor and we both love to laugh.

My father is very special. I am thankful that God gave him to me. And I wouldn't change that for anything else in the world.

Take a minute, and thank God for your father, wherever he may be or whatever kind of relationship you may have. God has given him to you to protect you and teach you. Thank God for all the things that he has taught you, and all the things that you enjoy together. Then go and tell him that you love him, and that you thank him for encouraging you to be who you are.

I love my papa, Daniel Whyte III,

Daniella

Thanks Danni, for your loving and encouraging words. This really means a lot to your old Papa because I know you mean them. I also want to thank all of my other daughters: Danita, Danielle, Danae`, Daniqua, and Danyelle, and all young black women everywhere, for being an inspiration to me to write this book. I love each one of you and May God bless you all.

P.T.:

♦ *"I cannot think of any need in childhood as strong as the need for a father's protection."*
—Sigmund Freud

♦ *"Be kind to thy father, for when thou were young, who loved thee so fondly as he? He caught the first accents that fell from thy tongue, and joined in thy innocent glee."*
—Margaret Courtney

♦ *"To a father growing old nothing is dearer than a daughter."*
—Euripides

♦ *"One father is more than a hundred schoolmasters."*
—George Herbert

BIBLE GEM: *"Children's children are the crown of old men; and the glory of children are their fathers."*
—Proverbs 17:6

TALK TO GOD: Holy Father, I thank You so much for the father that You have put in my life. Help me to learn all that I can from him. Help me to obey him, to love, and to care for him, even as he has done for me. I thank You for him. In Jesus' precious name. Amen.

BOOK: *They Call Me Dad: The Practical Art of Effective Fathering,* by Ken Canfield

CHECK IT OUT: www.fathers.com

Disclaimer on Quotations

Simply because we included a certain quotation in this book, does not necessarily mean that we condone the lifestyle or belief system of the person quoted. We included quotations in this book totally based upon the actual meaning of the words of the quotation and its connection to a particular chapter, and not upon the person who said it or wrote it.

THE MOTHERBOARD

This book was written from a male's point of view and I do believe that it is good for women to hear the truth from a male's point of view, from time to time. Of course, I also believe, according to the Scriptures, that the older women should teach the younger women. In light of that, I thought that it would be good to include, what we have called **the Motherboard**. These ministries below are directed by Godly women whom the Lord uses to teach other women.

Now, we are not connected to these ministries, and these ministries are not connected to our ministry, and I am sure that we might disagree on some fine points. But I am also confident that these women, and the ministries that they represent can assist you in getting the help that you need in any situation that you are facing; and if you are in need of a good, Bible-believing church in your area, I am sure they will be able to help you with that need as well. May God bless you and all young black women in America and around the world!

1. Mrs. Lois Evans
    The Urban Alternative
    www.loisevans.org

2. Mrs. Serita Jakes
    The Potter's House
    www.pottershouse.org

3. Mrs. June Hunt
    Hope For The Heart
    www.hopefortheheart.org

4. Mrs. Elisabeth Elliot
    Gateway to Joy
    www.elisabethelliot.org

5. Mrs. Joyce Meyer
    Joyce Meyer Ministries
    www.joycemeyer.org

6. Mrs. Vera McKissic
   Cornerstone Baptist Church
   www.cbc1983.org

7. Mrs. Betty Robison
   Life Today
   www.lifetoday.org

8. Mrs. Yvonne Capehart
   Sister Keeper Ministries International
   www.sisterkeeper.com

9. Mrs. Priscilla Shirer
   Priscilla Speaks Ministries
   www.priscillaspeaks.com

10. Mrs. Jeanette Baldwin
    COEBA
    www.coeba.org

11. Mrs. Joy Martin
    Joyful Christian Ministries
    www.joyfulchristianministries.com

12. Mrs. Shirley White
    Love Center Prayer & Counseling
    850-653-2203

13. **Focus on the Family**
    www.family.org

14. Mrs. Meriqua Whyte
    Daniella Whyte
    LYBW Ministries
    www.letterstoyoungblackwomen.org

15. Danita, Danae`, Daniqua, & Danyelle Whyte
    V-Girl Ministries (for ages 5-12)
    www.thevirtuousgirl.org

TOP 10 COLLEGES FOR YOUNG BLACK WOMEN

1. **Spelman College**
   Atlanta, GA
   404-681-3643
   www.spelman.edu

2. **Jarvis Christian College**
   Hawkins, TX
   903-769-5700
   www.jarvis.edu

3. **Pensacola Christian College**
   Pensacola, FL
   1-800-722-4636
   www.pcci.edu

4. **Bennett College**
   Greensboro, NC
   1-800-413-5323
   www.bennett.edu

5. **Bethune-Cookman College**
   Daytona Beach, FL
   386-481-2000
   www.cookman.edu

6. **Agnes Scott College**
   Decatur, GA
   1-800-868-8602
   www.agnesscott.edu

7. **Wesleyan College for Women**
   Macon, GA
   800-447-6610
   www.wesleyancollege.edu

8. **Fisk University**
   Nashville, TN
   1-800-433-FISK
   www.fisk.edu

9. **Florida A & M University**
   Tallahassee, FL
   850-599-3000
   www.famu.edu

10. **Texas Wesleyan University**
    Fort Worth, TX
    817-531-4444
    www.txwes.edu

If you need further assistance with understanding salvation or with your spiritual growth, please feel free to e-mail us at info@torchlegacy.com or call us at 1-877-TORCHLP